The Fall into Consciousness

J. Stanley Barlow is Associate Professor of Philosophy and Associate Dean of Faculty at Staten Island Community College in the City University of New York. His Ph.D. is from the University of St. Andrews in Scotland. In recent years he taught religion at Columbia University and served there as an academic administrator.

The Fall into

Consciousness

by J. STANLEY BARLOW

FORTRESS PRESS

Philadelphia

Library of Congress Catalog Card Number 72–87059

ISBN 0–8006–0136–x

3443H72   Printed in the United States of America   1-136

For Nell, Ann, David, Jim, and Susan

Contents

Preface

This book is my working out of a question which bothers a good
many of us, and I have addressed the essay to the general reader.
However, I have tried to select and present the materials in a way
that assures that the book can be useful as a text in courses on
religion and psychology and religion and culture, or in seminars
and discussion groups dealing with consciousness, freedom, and
responsibility. These topics are treated in the light of both the
dominant religious tradition of the West—theological "man talk"
—and the twentieth-century psychoanalytic movement.

Each chapter leads directly to the next, and the book is one
complete statement. Yet each chapter is a discussion within itself.

The first chapter raises the question of human consciousness,
first by looking afresh at one of the oldest of our culture's etiological stories, the Fall of Man in the Garden of Eden. Later, we
focus on a commonplace contemporary episode which illustrates the
difficulty in focusing on the "free" and "accountable" self. While
looking at this episode we introduce our panel of depth psychologists. They are selected carefully so as to give multiple light on
our question. The panel consists of Sigmund Freud, C. G. Jung,
Alfred Adler, Melanie Klein, Ronald Fairbairn, Otto Rank, Ian
Suttie, Karen Horney, Harry Stack Sullivan, Erik Erikson, and
certain others, who, like them, represent the practice of therapy.
And, along with this panel of therapists-theorists, the conversation
includes some representative theologians.

Unlike some studies that bring together psychology and religion,
this one tries to avoid a strictly Freudian or other single method.
If Freudians would say so and so, what would non-Freudians (like
Ian Suttie, for instance) say? What perhaps did Adler *see* that
Freud either overlooked or tended to underemphasize? On the
other hand, what Freudian insights might we lose if we should
simply follow Jung, Adler, or the so-called revisionists? Although
the treatment is critical it does not undertake to demolish any of

the schools of thought which are represented on the panel. I attempt to discern various angles of vision on the nature of human consciousness.

The narrative assumes that the reader already has some acquaintance with Western religion, that he has at some time in his life "gone to church" or thought about it and that he may occasionally try to relate his everyday thoughts about "human nature" to a view of himself and others as "creatures of God" or "members of the family of mankind," or some such lyric description of humanity. The book presupposes that the reader is not unfamiliar with the idea of confession and emotions that may be described as feelings of guilt, shame, or at least inadequacy. It assumes that he has not yet subjected his questions to systematic examination by the schools of psychology which are introduced here.

Some readers may come to a new appreciation of both the variety of thought within depth psychology and reasons for such variety. For some, the experience may go even further because the study does suggest ways in which different theories, even though they may be held tentatively, can be applied as a light on man and woman. Such exercises may enlarge one's understanding of himself.

The book was in preparation long before the publication of some recent works that seem to be relevant to the question which it addresses, such as Charles Reich's *The Greening of America,* with its "consciousness": "I," "II," and "III," and B. F. Skinner's *Beyond Freedom and Dignity.* Many others have written about depth psychology and religious or philosophical concerns. One thinks of such theorists—outside the profession of psychoanalyst —as Norman O. Brown, Philip Rieff, Herbert Marcuse, and Richard L. Rubenstein, who apply Freudian theory directly to the interpretation of history and use it to shape their own "doctrines" about culture. Although their work may be mentioned in passing, this essay will not engage them directly.

Because of the presence of women theorists on our panel and of Ian Suttie, who in the 1930's anticipated some of the quite recent counter-masculine corrective to Freudian theory, I hope that the consciousness discussed in this volume will demonstrate itself to be not exclusively that of the male—and of the female as she is understood by the male. But of this the reader will have to judge for *her*self since, alas, the statement was put together by a *him*self.

1

The Fall into Consciousness

The man and woman in the Garden of Eden wished to become wise, to attain the knowledge of good and evil. But getting such a prize proved to be too much for Adam and Eve. As we read this story in Genesis (chapters two and three) we cannot help being drawn into it. We can identify with all the characters, even the serpent!

The exit from the Garden corresponds to the experience of most of us. It carries the almost universal conviction: I am what I am by willing it so—even if I do not end up liking it. The eviction is from dependent harmony into enforced independence. "In the sweat of your face you shall eat bread. . . ." Such an awareness lives side by side with an attitude which tries to avoid guilt. This is in the story too. Adam refers to the determining influence of "The woman whom thou gavest to be with me. . . ." Eve blames the serpent. The serpent represents the fact that the cards are stacked against the human player anyway.

Yet the man was free to choose, says the story. He disobeyed an order—voluntarily. He is culpable—"No excuse, sir"—that is, if what he did was really wrong. There lurks a doubt about whether it was. Was the order not to eat of the tree of the knowledge of good and evil right? The serpent is the only one who is outspoken against it. However, the narrator leaves some doubt as to his own opinion. Would the human be human without what this story calls the knowledge of good and evil? Of course it may be that a cynical note is struck too: humanity may be one grand mistake.

The serpent seems to act the role of a reasonable creature when he voices for Eve what surely ought to be the human's grievance against the fate decreed if he should eat of that fruit. Surely the penalty is out of all proportion to the offense. "Did God say . . .?" He must be trying to hold man under, to deny him any further development. Surely the command is selfish in the extreme. God

1

is like an Oriental despot. The serpent urges Eve to break her bondage to ignorance by eating the fruit, ". . . you will be like God, knowing good and evil."

Perhaps the story is meant to read backwards: We are deprived of the benefits of paradise simply because we tried to be ourselves, knowing good and evil—knowing.

This is how the author sees the actual lot of humanity. As the personality develops out of early infancy, it seems to be urged from within and also from without to realize its own individual destiny, to grow in knowledge, to conquer the world through knowledge.

The story may reflect the transition of society from the food-gathering economy, and also, from the hunting economy (garments of skins were made for Adam and Eve), to the economy of the farmer and herdsman. However, the narrator represents this later economy, and he seems to focus his psychological concern on the individual as he tries to understand the meaning of the life cycle.

To be sure, the storyteller is reshaping materials from even earlier traditions of folktale. His story becomes a statement of theology, of anthropology, of psychology. It is a kind of lament, an etiological myth about how we got here in this state. The gate through which we came is knowledge.

Ian Suttie calls the process "psychic weaning." Sigmund Freud sees it as a progression of crises which are like stairs from birth to adulthood. The crucial landing is what he calls the resolution of the Oedipus crisis. Otto Rank sees the process as the emergence of the individual will through becoming first a counter-will.

The Garden of Eden allegory ties up all the evils of our existence with the fact of death. Man can choose between continuing in a kind of post-natal, even fetal, stupor and becoming conscious of his relative independence and responsibility (knowing good and evil). To be *homo cogitans* he must pay the price of lonely suffering and death. In other words, his fall, if we must call it that, is a fall into consciousness. To exist is to exist, but to know that you exist is to know that you die.

As it is appropriated by Christianity the story of the fall of Adam emerges as a part of a new optimism. "As in Adam all die," says the Apostle Paul, "even so in Christ shall all be made alive." The "sin" of Adam—and of all of us—is overcome in Christ. It is tempting, at this point, for us to speculate about what the inner meaning of such a faith can be in terms of consciousness. Is the Christian notion of paradise regained a return to the state before the fall into consciousness, or may it be an entrance into a new kind of consciousness (not to be equated necessarily with "Consciousness III"—as propounded by Charles Reich,[1] nor the Walden Two type imagined by B. F. Skinner,[2] nor conceptions of awareness which we meet in the literature of Jainism, Buddhism, and Vedanta, although all of these can be relevant to our inquiry)?

Much has been said in the long history of theology about what that fall of Adam was. St. Augustine saw it as a fall from rational control of one's will into sensual irrationality—concupiscence. The sixteenth-century reformers renewed the voice of Augustine. Characteristically, Luther described "the bondage of the will." Adam fell into bondage to a new master. Prototypal man's personality was twisted away from its true center in the good. Like the hero in pre-Christian Greek tragedy, Adam—primal man— overreached himself and assumed prerogatives that are beyond him.

In this book we shall let modern depth psychologists do most of the talking about this phenomenon we have called "the fall into consciousness." At times one is tempted to baptize them and make them theologians, so reminiscent of theology are their concerns and methods of discourse. Nevertheless, we shall regard them as what they like to be, clinicians, who, however, have the habit of extrapolating, sometimes quite considerably, from their data.

If we take the story of Adam and Eve in the Garden as a parable or mirror for the experience of all mankind, we have to go further and appreciate the variety which the "fall" into consciousness can take. Granted, this fall is actually more of an ascent—a heightening of awareness. Yet, the awareness is peculiar to each Adam, each Eve.

1. *The Greening of America* (New York: Random House, 1970).
2. *Walden Two* (New York: Macmillan, 1948). Cf. Skinner, *Beyond Freedom and Dignity* (New York: Alfred A. Knopf, 1971).

We usually assume that for each one there is an executive self, that within one which says "I." Yet it is no simple task to try to focus on this ego, to understand it, to be fair to it as we reflect on ethics, esthetics, education, politics, and religion—the whole gamut of Adam's arts and sciences! In other words, what in Eve said yes to the serpent? What in the man said yes to Eve? What in the narrator-theologian takes upon himself—and upon all mankind—the onus of responsibility?

Sigmund Freud, as psychoanalyst, listened to and talked with adult Adams and Eves—his youngest Adam was little Hans, so far as we know. Every patient was on the east of Eden, outside looking in and trying to cope with existence outside paradise. Alfred Adler, who departed from the Freudian circle of faith and developed his own psychology, worked with children and adults. C. G. Jung, another defector from Freudianism, a seasoned psychiatrist even when he first entered the movement, relied heavily upon his own work with schizophrenics to conclude that the individual's sense of ego is but part of a much larger phenomenon: his consciousness is but a speck of terrain on a largely submerged island in a vast sea of human reality. Jung's psychology may serve as a kind of bridge to the East and even to Western mystical ways of posing the religious question about the meaning of consciousness. Other depth psychologists have followed these three, working alongside them, or over against them, and nowadays increasingly eclectically in their wake. All of them are busy suggesting ways of making the wilderness more like a garden, or, at least, the responsibility less onerous and morbid. Of course, these and all psychotherapists, large though their numbers be, are but a fraction of the therapeutically concerned. In a sense, everyone is a physician—his own anyway. The myriad salvation religions of the world, which include the varieties of Judaism, Islam, Christianity, and Hinduism, Buddhism, Taoism, and tribal cults, address themselves to the problem of painful consciousness in the individual.

Consciousness presupposes a subject of consciousness, the I in "I am conscious." Although they are especially known for their emphasis on unconscious forces in the individual, the depth psychologies address themselves to this question: What is the nature of that I, what is the structure of the ego? Furthermore, the unconscious with them is a positive category. In other words, practically speaking, it is a kind of consciousness! Thus, Freud had to explain his concept of ego as the executive self which extends into the unconscious—indeed it grows up out of it. Jung talks of the persona, the animus/anima, the ego and the shadow: he emphasizes the complexity of what we are accustomed to call the self— the ego can never serve as synonym for it. Yet, even for Jung, the ego is of critical importance.

If there is something in a person that looks out upon the world, reacts consciously, and "unconsciously," to it, thinks of it as related somehow to one's own existence, and that tries to make the best of that existence and to take on at least a measure of responsibility, then what precisely is that something, the I of responsibility?

Now, in order to carry our inquiry forward, or at least to illustrate the complexity of the question, I shall relate and comment upon an incident, poignant, though commonplace—when we think of the abundance of material produced in recent years by the tragedy of Vietnam and other scenes of inhumanity. In telling of the incident, which I witnessed on a Boston subway some years ago, I shall introduce some of the members of our panel, the various schools of depth psychology which offer light on our question.

One sees a frightful altercation, a one-sided attack, in a public place. A man in sudden rage knocks another down and unconcious. He continues to pound and kick his victim until the slowly alerted passers-by force a halt. He then turns on them, with his fists clenched. Like Goliath, he is ready to take on anyone else. What is going on in his inner world? His victim is innocent. Why has the man-in-rage chosen one of the crowd and assaulted him so viciously?

The psychiatrist Harry Stack Sullivan introduced the concept of parataxic distortion, which is kin to the Freudian idea of projection. The man-in-rage is seeing things! True, his pent-up rage can cite a wisp of a provocation in the victim's earlier mild retort or rebuke at his loud behavior. But the victim cannot as himself mean this much to his attacker. He is attacked not as he is in himself but as he is as an object which represents some threatening presence already in the aggressor's own world. The victim is seen through the distorted lens, the peculiar constructs of the attacker. This troubled inner world, or mind, of the aggressor, in its inability to contain itself, externalizes its conflict and casts in the role of villain the handiest person-object present. To the attacker the victim seems to be the agent of a hostile power. "Parataxic distortion" is seeing things in terms of one's own peculiar experience. Borrowing from the terminology of grammar, Sullivan described as syntaxic the objective sequences of things or events as they are. Prototaxic impressions are the kind which the infant gets during the stage when objects and events seem to him to be unrelated. Later, even after early infancy, objects and events may seem to be unrelated or distorted in their relationship or arrangement in place and time. Such distortions are called "parataxic." "Subjective" may be quite adequate as a descriptive in many cases. However, it does not carry the connotation of pathogenesis which such a violent incident as this one suggests to us.

Yet even after we have granted such a description of this attack upon an innocent person, how can we get at the rage, its intensity, its obviously murderous goal? This kind of question seems to express the reason for one's dwelling on such an incident long after he witnesses it.

There can be no doubt, in this instance, that the man-in-rage is actually in the process of destroying his victim when he is forced to stop. An elderly woman, one of the more courageous of those near the fray, calls for an immediate halt to this senseless pounding of a victim who may already be dead as far as the crowd can see.

"You have no right to do that," is the almost curious refrain. Yet, how profound a judgment! It speaks of the more syntaxic valuation of this encounter of two worlds. No one has the right to hit another, especially when he is down, and never without just cause—whatever that is: perhaps it is a provocation syntaxically commensurate with the reflexive retaliation. "You have no right;

you are not justified in tearing down the investment of others; the person of another is not yours to destroy. How can you presume to destroy that which is not yours even to touch?" These are the judgments of the, alas, too weakly protective onlookers—the random chorus for this happening, the ad hoc social milieu for the aggressor and his victim.

But the attacker seems not to be asking such questions. His rage is saying to all the world, "I am destroying this person-object. I am ready to turn my asserted right-to-destroy upon you!" Here is the acting out of a might-is-right doctrine, however irrational the articulation. Here is an example of the problem of evil, what we have usually called moral evil.

Yet to his own parataxic vision, the man-in-rage is destroying a bad and threatening object. At least this is what most depth psychologists seem to be saying. Threatening, in what sense? To whom? Or to what? Even if we take into consideration the biochemical effects of alcohol, drugs, or narcotics, even if we allow for the neurological tensions created by these or by some natural organic disturbance, even if the incident has some glandular determinants, we nevertheless must recognize that in the "thinking" of the man-in-rage the threat is conceived by his whatever-conceives-of-things as something directed against his own inner strivings, his own struggling, perhaps self-despised self. He defends himself.

To say that he manifests hostility, that his action bespeaks hatred, is true enough. But what is hostility? Why is it? Here depth psychology has more than one answer. Yet there seems to be a concerted light in the very recognition of the inner dynamics involved.

Sigmund Freud eventually posed as explanation a primitive death instinct in the human organism. The urge to destroy operates as a part of the given with all the force of a need within the human organism. It may be conceived as resistance to change, an urge to return to earlier stages of development, eventually to dust.

It may be more than merely analogous to the destructiveness of the lion as it stalks its prey, falls upon and devours it. It may have been part of the survival equipment in the cave man's makeup. Destroy to survive!

Certainly some such theory of an instinct of destructiveness seems to be the simplest explanation. Society's task vis-à-vis crimes of passion becomes almost solely that of controlling and channelling the ineradicable aggressive instincts of humans. Against the apostle we may have to say with increasing insight, "Exercise profiteth much!" Contrived outlets for aggression must be improved and made available to all.

The hypothesis of a primitive drive to destroy is regarded variously, even by Freud's own disciples. Yet all depth psychologists recognize the phenomenon of human aggressiveness. Most of them regard destructiveness as a synthetic impulse. It may be derived from more primitive urges that flow together towards some wrong, perhaps clinically correctable, goal. The compulsive aspect of rage and hostile aggression is recognized by all depth psychologists.

What seems to get lost is the focus of accountability. As we approach a focus we lose the accountability. Who commits sin? In our street attack incident the readiest answer is the aggressor. Where would society be if this were not the answer? But who is the aggressor, what in him is the I of accountability? It is precisely here, as we enter the strange world of his kaleidoscopic selfhood, that we get lost. He as a responsible self, a free moral agent, all but dissolves before our search. Yet if we withdraw again to the outside where we observe him leave off battering his victim, we see an apparent unity, a man, reluctantly desisting, facing around to the crowd, much in the manner of a trapped animal. His clenched fists, after a long moment, fall. He heads for the nearest exit. Who drops his fists? Who heads toward freedom from the eyes of the crowd? Freudians say the ego, the agency of reason, recovers control after a momentary loss of it to the surging forces of the biological organism—the *id*—perhaps allied with the destructive superego (the I that hates the I), which is built around the introjected bad—threatening—parent. These irrational powers had stormed the capitol and overthrown the executive ego. Then, after the coup d'etat, when the aggressive energy has about spent itself for awhile, and the reproving crowd effectively delivers a counter-stimulus to the man's psyche, there is a restoration of ego control. Obviously, this man's ego is relatively weak, possibly badly divided or split.

Karen Horney, Harry Stack Sullivan, and others among the revisionists, or neo-Freudians, as they are sometimes called, would say that it is the "actual self" (Horney) or "waking self" (Sullivan) that leaves off beating the victim, after some kind of coup and restoration.

Carl G. Jung would say that it is the conscious ego—with its persona, or face to the world—after a violent eruption of unconscious drives in assertion of the unconscious. There has been a frantic, disoriented attempt within the man-in-rage to deflect on to an outside object the assault which the ego itself experiences from within. The outside world becomes the surrogate enemy for the inner forces of rebellion. After all, the societal environment actually shapes the persona in relative violation of the inner, endopsychic, life. This has been an incident in the painful process of the individual's dynamic selfhood, his psyche's unceasing struggle to become integrated.

Alfred Adler would see it as a failure to arrive at a socially approved means of asserting oneself against the feeling of inferiority. The now-prone victim has been appropriated by his aggressor's fear of inferiority or of the failure to be superior. The man-in-rage has struck out against that fear of failure. At the same time he has made a pathetic bid for some kind of social recognition of his fiction of superiority.

Ego psychologists among the Freudians, like Erik H. Erikson, may describe this incident in terms of a prolonged crisis of identity when there is intense need to repudiate.

The so-called "English School" of Freudians—who are often distinguished from the so-called "ego psychologists"—led by Melanie Klein, would say that this is likely an infantile attempt to rid the inner world of a bad object which it had introjected (internalized). This acting out is an attempt to eject an inner persecutor. The persecutor stands for death. Death by mutilation. The victim is merely a screen upon which the aggressor projects his own color slide of the "bad mother," perhaps the cannibalistic images retained from infancy, a "bad object" which carries the threat of extinction. Even as a child smashes a toy which has suddenly been vested with evil, so the aggressor tries to smash the innocent victim.

Sullivan would agree that the victim is experienced, through parataxic distortion, as the bad mother—or bad father, bad sibling, bad peer, bad "significant person." Horney could see the victim as being cast in the role of the shaming, rejecting social environment against which the fearful child rages.

Probing further into the intrapsychic etiology of this aggressive act, the Freudians could probably relate the act to the aggressor's narcissism. Since the man-in-rage has been heard before the incident to proclaim loudly, "I am going to destroy myself," there is added reason to suspect that the victim does actually represent something close to, or substitutive for, the aggressor's own self-image. Is not the destructiveness of an object likely to be self-destructiveness, which suddenly veers away from the self outward to an object in sight? What makes it veer? It is the residual self-love, the primary narcissism, reinforced by secondary narcissism (emotional attachment to one's own body). To Freudians, the self-concept is derived directly from one's own body-concept as it is formed through experience in early childhood.

Hence a kind of self-concern forces the rage outward to the near destruction of an innocent person. Then the threat which is represented by the disapproving onlookers alerts the same primary self-love to spare the victim any further destruction.

Who then is the aggressor? It is the impersonal, misshapen, chaotic aggregation of somatic energy which forces its way through the censor controls of the socially aware, waking self. Who is the victim? He is a substitute for the aggressor's own self-concept.

Representative of the kind of understanding which depth psychology seeks in viewing any such incident may be the following reconstruction of the event, based on the method of Ian Suttie. Suttie died before his collection of papers, *The Origins of Love and Hate,* was published in 1935.[3] He formed no circle of disci-

3. Ian D. Suttie, *The Origins of Love and Hate* (London: Kegan Paul, 1935).

ples, although he has influenced such writers as John Macmurray, the Scottish moral philosopher, and Ashley Montagu, the social anthropologist. For our purpose we shall place Suttie among the schools of thought which make up our panel. Although he was hardly given a hearing by most Freudians, this independent, respected British psychiatrist shaped his theories against those of Freud, Adler, and Jung—but especially Freud.

According to Suttie, love is prototypically the love of the mother for her child and the child's reciprocal love. Rooted biologically in the symbiotic relationship of parent organism with offspring, it is the basis of all future relationships for the child. Rage and hatred are derived, although negatively, from the experience of love. The venting of rage is in its prototype a device, however distorted and violent, for getting attention. In this, Suttie seems to agree somewhat with the Adlerians, of whom Rudolph Dreikurs is an important recent spokesman. However, Suttie says, the intention of the child-in-rage is not to gain recognition and a sense of power, as the Adlerians say; it is simply to try to win back the love which he feels he has lost. Hence, his fear of having been abandoned by the source of love, cut off from the nourishment of his social self, results in rage and hatred—which is directed rage. Therefore, with the Johannine writer in the New Testament and also with Oskar Pfister, the Freudian pastor-psychoanalyst of Zurich, and with Professor Macmurray, and with a host of present-day psychologists and others, Suttie regards the fundamental polarity as not that of love and hatred, but of love and fear. Hatred is derived from fear; specifically, the fear of losing or of being unable to regain love.

The attention that a child craves is of course, that of his mother or mother substitute. The emotional drama in the background is typically that of the displaced infant's attack upon the mother, hence, society, and her suckling infant, the usurper, the sibling, or sibling substitute. The fundamental desire of the child-in-rage is to be restored to the good graces of his mother. Otto Rank, Sullivan, Erich Fromm, even Freud, each in his own way, among depth psychologists, and Paul Tillich, notably, among recent theologians, stress reunion as a goal—if not the goal—to which the human being aspires.

Is the brutal pounding and kicking of an already prostrate

victim in some sense a bid for the crowd to pay attention to the actor, for society whose prototype is "mother" to put down her other nurslings and pick him up? Is this not the story of Cain and Abel? Is not the victim here the aggressor's brother-image Abel? Cain, or sibling jealousy, as Suttie phrased it, is a paradigm of hatred. Actually, however, it is love unrequited, simply trying to remove what it sees as the obstacle to the restoration of love. The sibling is hated never for what he is in himself but only for what he is as an obstacle.

Jealous rage is attention getting and love seeking. Certainly the loud, exhibitionist behavior of the aggressor before he strikes down his victim lends credibility to the suggestion that he is bidding for the crowd's attention, although obviously his inner construct or image of that crowd is distorted. Is the distortion backward, looking toward the primal image of the mother, or the nurturing environment? Is he acting out a nursery scene, snatching the hated sibling image from the mother's embrace as in the fantasy of the child who smashes a toy, saying to the mother by his action: "I do not want you-and-him or you-and-toys; I want you! With me in your arms where he is instead! Can't you see? I am smashing it, smashing it, smashing it!"

Destoying sibling images and toys can be a substitute for getting satisfaction from the mother. It can be distorted substitute behavior for the very pattern of play which she has introduced in her effort to wean the child. Some may see special significance in the fact that the attacker's compulsive kicking was directed at the victim's mouth. Yet, we may relate this also, perhaps primarily, to the fact that the victim had spoken to the attacker. Perhaps his mild rebuke had been construed as not merely verbal lashing but as the verbal rejection the aggressor had come to expect from "mother" and from society.

In the example of a man-in-rage attacking an innocent victim, we witness passions that are overreaching, to be sure. It could be used to illustrate many a theologian's formulation for sin, including Reinhold Niebuhr's in *The Nature and Destiny of Man*.[4] The aggressor has pre-empted the place of God (or whatever) in taking

4. Reinhold Niebuhr, *The Nature and Destiny of Man* (New York: Charles Scribner's Sons, 1941–).

authority over the very life and death of the victim. By his act of knocking him down, beating and pounding him, he arbitrarily is determining the victim's destiny. He decides whether he shall keep teeth in his head, whether his brain will be damaged, his ribs broken, and, except for the forceful intervention of the onlookers, he is deciding whether he shall continue to breathe. The crowd's voice, "You have no right" expresses a judgment and will which contravene, indeed transcend, those of the actor.

Examples may be cited which change *dramatis personae*. We think of My Lai, and of lynching episodes, of racial violence, mob action, genocide, where the crowd-in-rage or a whole society-in-rage rationalizes its rage as a concern for a brand of "justice." The crowd and the collective may pre-empt the place of God.

In the example we have used, the area of responsibility eludes us when we try to bring it to focus within the psyche of the aggressor. Who struck the victim? A man whose reasoning will or ego may well have had no control over his actions. Who dropped his fists and went away? It was the same man whose reasoning will had been forced back into control either by his primary self-love or some inner principle of self-preservation that may defy such a simple description. A law at work within him finally overcame another law enough for him to make his staggering way out of the crowd and away from the victim. That law which did the suppressing may simply have been fear of the consequences, what Freudians call the law of reality, the reality principle.

The depth psychologists on our panel generally agree that the executive self is that to which therapy must appeal. Psychotherapy is ego therapy. Yet it does not take a Ronald D. Laing to point out to us that effective therapy must somehow reach beyond the rational will of the patient or client. Psychotherapy is also id therapy. Where there is "irresponsible" behavior as in the example we have described, a realistic, responsible subject-self is not in control. Hence, in all the theories we find the same difficulty in any attempt to bring to a focus the accountable self. At the same time, depth psychology reads in a way that encourages us to formulate an instrumentalistic conception which makes of guilt-feeling—or the capacity for feeling guilty—a capacity for assuming responsibility and centeredness "before God and man."

2

The I in "I am Conscious"

Sigmund Freud developed a theory or, perhaps we should say, a model of the psyche, in which the ego tries to assume a responsible attitude toward both the outside world and the world of whirling drives within. His daughter, Anna, contributed to Freudian ego psychology by elaborating the notion of ego mechanisms. The ego assimilates what it can and defends itself against what it cannot readily manage.

Freud was not the first to liken the human being to a horse and rider. In his *New Introductory Lectures,* Freud says: "One might compare the relation of the ego to the id with that between a rider and his horse. The horse provides the locomotive energy, and the rider has the prerogative of determining the goal and of guiding the movements of his powerful mount towards it." But all too often the picture is of the less ideal situation, when "the rider is obliged to guide his horse in the direction in which it itself wants to go."[1]

John Calvin, in sixteenth-century Geneva, quotes St. Augustine of Hippo comparing the human will to a horse as it is being mounted. The devil and God are the riders. "'If God mounts, he, like a temperate and skillful rider, guides it calmly, urges it when too slow, reins it in when too fast, curbs its forwardness and overaction, checks its bad temper, and keeps it on the proper course,' he says. 'But if the devil has seized the saddle, like an ignorant and rash rider, he hurries it over broken ground, drives it into ditches, dashes it over precipices, spurs it into obstinacy or fury.'"[2]

Socrates, speaking in Plato's *Phaedrus,* describes the nature of the "soul" (psyche)—although ". . . her true form be ever a theme

---

1. "The Anatomy of the Mental Personality," trans. W. J. H. Sprott (New York: W. W. Norton & Co., Inc., 1933), pp. 82–112.
2. *Institutes of the Christian Religion,* trans. Henry Beveridge (Grand Rapids: William B. Eerdmans Pub. Co., 1953), II, iv, 1, Vol. 1, pp. 265–66.

of large and more than mortal discourse. . . ." The metaphor is composite: "a pair of winged horses and a charioteer. . . . the human charioteer drives his in a pair; and one of them is noble and of noble breed, and the other is ignoble and of ignoble breed; and the driving of them of necessity gives a great deal of trouble to him. . . ."[3]

Freud, Calvin, Augustine, Plato are all speaking psychologically. Both Freud and the Greek philosophers are placing the dualism within the psyche, while the Christian theologians place it in external rivals for the reins of the human will. In Freud's view, the ego may be skillful enough to control the id, but often it simply goes along for the ride. In his theory of psychic or mental mechanisms—ego mechanisms—the figure is less that of horse and rider and more that of simply one or the other: the intelligent organism which interacts with the environment. Perhaps analogies may be used like an engineer operating complicated machinery or a government trying to manage a nation. The mechanisms are ego (ego defense) devices as the organism manages to maintain and control itself in a world it cannot control.

Yet the ego of Freudian man seems to act automatically, according to the rules which the mechanisms imply. Whatever freedom there may be is circumscribed indeed. The ego's freedom seems to be like that of unconscious life, the freedom to be what it is determined to be. Man's sense of ego is slowly mutating toward having conscious strength to withstand the encroachment of the society and culture until it is fulfilled. Alas, according to some theorists, that fulfillment can be reduced simply to achievement of heterosexual or sublimational satisfaction, after which it withers and dies in its own good time.

Freud insists on the multiple ties that bind the rational to the irrational and the spiritual to the somatic in the individual. He strives to avoid the dichotomy of soul (psyche) and body (soma). The psyche is somatic. True, both are described perhaps too mechanistically by this theorist whose vocabulary of metaphors reflects his late ninteenth-century orientation to both physiology

3. "Phaedrus," in *The Dialogues of Plato*, trans. B. Jowett (New York: Random House, 1937), Vol. 1, p. 250.

and therapy. Yet, some of his present-day followers try to hold fundamentally to his model and psychogenesis but with some modulation away from the severe mechanistic tendency. They are intent on preserving the derivation of the psyche from the soma, within the natural history of the species. And man in relation to other men is soma encountering other somata.

According to Freud, and to his colleague Karl Abraham, an individual develops through traumatic experiences or crises. He is characterized by his erotic attachments enroute to adulthood. The first crisis is birth itself. Psychogenesis proceeds according to the following crisis stages: oral, anal-urethral, phallic—for both boys and girls, climaxing in the Oedipus situation or complex—and genital, which is separated from the phallic stage by a long period of latency, which corresponds to later childhood and pre-adolescence. After years of trying to assimilate the trauma of the Oedipal situation, the individual at last achieves suitable hetero-sexual patterns of adjustment and healthy, or socially acceptable, outlets, that is, if all goes well. To achieve such success, the person's ego must be relatively strong, with relatively smoothly working mechanisms, including, notably, sublimation.

Early Freud taught that the genesis of the adult psyche was governed by two laws or principles: pleasure and reality. The ego serves under the reality principle but with a mandate to allow as much pleasure as the outside world will permit. The ego is the aspect of the organism that registers the balance between these two principles. Indeed, the painful denial of pleasure by the environ-ment has been the cause of the organism's awareness of reality.

Each crisis is the height of the tension between pleasure and reality at a certain stage in the development of organismic (somatic) man. "Good" means satisfaction. "Evil" is the want or denial of satisfaction. Ego control is relative success in the over-coming of such evil with such good. This may be simply by holding back the good—defined hedonistically—until it can be *real*ized. The feeling of pain can be projected and thus vested in outside objects, which may, in fact, be quite neutral. At the same time, outside evil may be introjected destructiveness. Hostility may be projected pain.

Freud's later theory saw each developmental crisis as combining reality outside the person with the conflictual reality within. Pleasure and destructiveness are usually in some kind of alliance as the organism confronts its natural and social environment. The environmental forces interact, being allied variously with the two inner groupings of impulses: eros and destructiveness. The ego, according to Freud's later theory, is eros-seeking but reality-aware, as the executive within the human organism. It has long since surrendered a part of its domain to the oppressive outside ego— the image of parents, particularly the father figure. The internalized outside-ego is called the superego. This, for Freud, is the seat of what is popularly called conscience. According to Freud, this part of the self is in the service of destructiveness, rather than love, and its target is the ego. Hence, the conscience is the internalized persecutor of the ego.

Surely whatever made Freud develop his saga of love and death has been kin to that which exercised the minds of theologians like Calvin, Luther, Augustine, and Paul when they saw a destructive opposition to life affecting the human consciousness. We should extend the comparisons to ancient gnosticism and Iranian religion —Zoroastrianism and its derivatives—since dualism is a definitive feature of such religions: the human situation is a part of a cosmic warfare between light and darkness, good and evil, the true and the false.

The human organism's last judgment—or crisis—is death. The life instinct finally surrenders to the death instinct, thus proving the superior strength of the latter. According to the death instinct theory, the dead weight of basic matter (the inertia of matter) pulls the aspiring creature down to the grave. Freud's reverence for the superior death instinct seems at times to tempt him away from the eros-thanatos[4] dualism to a pessimistic monism in which he all but defines life in terms of death. Perhaps the life instinct, too, is derived ultimately from the resistance which matter offers to the forces that try to shape it. Yet there is a kind of hope, cheer-

---

4. We should note that Freud himself avoided using the Greek word for the death instinct. Some of his followers, notably Melanie Klein, use the term "thanatos."

ing for eros, in much of Freud's writing. The logic of Freudian psychotherapy, itself, generally seems to favor the life forces.

Some depth psychologists depart altogether from the model which Freudians use to recount the development of the psyche. Others alter it considerably. Yet each suggests some model for the self.

C. G. Jung sees the psyche as being in a continual state of development. He moves his lens away from early childhood and adolescence and their fulfillment in adulthood, and focuses on the middle years. He emphasizes that a major and sometimes creative change often takes place in middle life, when the latent self emerges and often reverses former conscious patterns of thought, many of which have been false to the inner self in the interest of getting along with the outside world. In later adulthood, the partially misconstrued pressures of society become weaker in relative strength against the pent inner forces—the libido as *élan vital*.

Alfred Adler views the self as developing through three major crises: we may take the words, *love, vocation,* and *community* as identifying the crises. Of course, Adler, unlike Freud, avoids trying to construe the personality in multiple structures (ego, superego, id). He tries to see the psyche and organism as a unity, somewhat like the reasoning will as expounded by Otto Rank after his break with Freud. Adler's psychology tends to simplify the problem of human consciousness and human striving. The goal for the small child is superiority. Healing brings to the individual a reformation in his inner economics, with the replacing of the fictional goal of superiority with the realistic goal of community (power transformed into cooperation).

Unlike Jung and Adler, the most notable early defectors from Freud, Ian Suttie makes his penetrating critique from outside the movement. He directs his intellectual artillery at the so-called Oedipal conflict. Suttie suggests that "Laius jealousy" and "Cain jealousy" are at least equally appropriate for describing certain manifestations in child-parents-sibling relationships. According to the Greek legend, Laius had tried to kill his son Oedipus in infancy. Perhaps the male child senses actual Laius-like envy in his father, which is not to be explained simply by the theories of projection and introjection of hostility and a regressive Oedipal feeling in the father which projects his own father's image onto his small son. It is even conceivable that the theorist who is attracted by the Oedipus reductionism is being motivated by his own Laius feelings toward his sons and his younger colleagues. We have already discussed Suttie's theory of Cain, or sibling, jealousy. Cain in jealous rage killed his brother Abel because Yahweh preferred the offering which the younger had brought (Genesis, chapter four).

Perhaps the social crisis is that of psychic weaning, as Suttie says, when the child envies every person or object which takes any of the mother's attention. Most parents of young children and others who tend them can attest to the frequency of such jealousy.

Harry Stack Sullivan bypasses such difficulties as attend the use of myth versus myth in his outline of the development of the "self system." The stages are as follows: (1) infancy, from birth to the maturation of the capacity for language behavior, (2) childhood, to the maturation of the capacity for living with compeers, (3) juvenile, to the maturation of the capacity for intimacy with one's own sex, "isophilic intimacy," (4) pre-adolescence, to the maturation of the capacity for intimacy with a member of the other sex, (5) early adolescence, to the patterning of "lustful behavior," (6) late adolescence, to maturity in heterosexual adjustment, (7) adulthood.[5]

Sullivan preserves both the somatic and the hedonistic criteria which are so important in Freudian theory. His outline of stages along life's way suggests his gauge for emotional health. "Interpersonal" is the key concept with him. Since to him persons are living somata, interpersonal is interorganismic. The self-system is formed by these stages and is determined by the milieu and the organism's two goals: security and satisfaction.

To Sullivan, the "waking self" and the "self system" of which it is a part are produced through a continual interaction of the organism with its environment.

5. "The Meaning of Anxiety in Psychiatry and in Life," *Psychiatry*, XI, 1 (1948), p. 5. Also, *Conceptions of Modern Psychiatry*, 2nd ed. (New York: W. W. Norton & Co., Inc., 1953), pp. 30–56.

Among the Freudians the same kind of insight seems to be present in the theory of Melanie Klein. Formerly of Berlin, later of London, she is regarded as an original thinker within the fold. Yet her theories are controversial even among Freudians. She shocked the world of psychoanalysis with papers, followed in 1927 by a book, on the psychoanalysis of children. Freud had taught that psychoanalysis was possible only with subjects who had passed the Oedipal crisis and become possessed of a superego. The therapeutic agent is the analyst's parent-role. The analyst undertakes to re-form the too oppressive superego (internalized parent). True to the Freudian model, Klein tried to remove the anomaly by pushing the ontogenesis of the superego back to the oral stage. Not the father, but the mother's breast—the hated breast—is the nucleus of the superego. The loved breast is, as with Freud, the first good object.

A colleague in Edinburgh, another original thinker in the Freudian larger circle, was W. Ronald Fairbairn, who has made much of the notion of the splitting of the ego. The ego is a host of egos corresponding to the many introjected objects. "I am all my objects!" This is reminiscent of the pervasive karma which binds the jiva (soul) throughout, weighting it down with material experience—in the philosophy of Jainism. Fairbairn does posit a central ego which tries to maintain order. His theories complement Klein's by laying even greater stress on the process of object-cathexis and image-splitting. To be sure, there are important differences between the two theorists. Fairbairn declined to follow Freud on the matter of instinctual dualism, while Klein, in her own way, used the death-instinct hypothesis. Fairbairn focused on the object itself, within the psychology of ego-and-its-objects. He prefers not to rest his conception of what is happening on the supposed instinctual energies at play among those objects. It is the child's image of its objects which gives definition to the child's own multifarious ego.

Klein's view seems to be that the twin mechanisms of introjection and projection effect the construction of the superego and the ego, building them substantially out of the objects experienced from the moment of birth, if not earlier. In effect, the ego becomes a world of objects organized by eros and thanatos. Thanatos-controlled images are the inner persecutors, the bad mother, bad father, bad objects that give imagery and symbol to the cause of death and destruction. Fairbairn calls these forces the inner saboteur. The good objects, split images of those objects experienced in the subject's contact with the outside world, are the life-images, the symbols of love, goodness, purposiveness: the good breast, the good mother, and goodness!

The infant realm depicted by Klein and her collaborators is fascinating and suggestive of profound insight. Despite her sometimes perplexing anthropomorphisms she presents the reader with a concept of ego which is at least as complex as the world of objects which it encounters along its formative way, and which satisfy, tease, threaten, and give pain.

Like Klein and Erich Fromm, Karen Horney studied under Freud's disciple and collaborator, Karl Abraham, in Berlin. She came to America and found her own school of psychoanalysis, refusing ever to abandon the term. Indeed she continued for years to be listed as a member of the International Association of Psychoanalysts. She openly rejected Freud's instinctual dualism, refuted his psychology of woman, arguing cogently against the notion of female Oedipal and penis envy. She refused the ego-id-superego trinity as erroneously conceived and proposed another trinity: self, personality structure, and trends, and still another, in describing the self, as "actual self," "ideal self," and "real self." By the time she wrote her last book, in 1950, she was using this tri-focal description of the self. True, all three foci can be loosely correlated with the ego-superego, but it would be difficult to find a place for the Freudian id.

Horney likens the "ideal self" to Freud's earlier idea of an ego ideal. Also, it is like Adler's "self ideal." The "actual self" is the pilot self, according to Horney. It is the self at the helm in the storm of life, steering according to whatever guidance it gets from charts and weather. The "ideal self" is that which the actual self is convinced by his social environment that he ought to be. Emotional illness and character disorders result from the imposition of an unrealistic ideal self image on the individual. The "real self" is the self which is possible of fulfillment. In positing this concept, Horney expresses her hopeful outlook. She is a liberal, melioristic, humanistic theologian in believing that the person is essentially good. Evil comes from the storm of life and from the negative results of other persons' anxieties, the oppressive ideals which are relativistic and self-seeking in the worst sense. Against the actual, which cannot be avoided, and against the false ideal, which may be cured, psychotherapy should evoke, nourish, and support the "real" in the patient.

Horney sees the early formative years as important but not all important in the development and ongoing life of the self. They establish a pattern. However, an adult's problems are his present interpersonal ones. They are not simply a regression to unresolved problems of early childhood. Sullivan's view of the self has the same flexibility. Certainly Adler's does. The existential analysts— Ludwig Binswanger, Rollo May, and others—and also the transactional analysts stress the now in the life of the Subject. We have noted Jung's view of a never-ending psychogenesis.

Jung depicts a microcosmic psyche: the conscious and the unconscious. To him, the deep unconscious is racial or collective. It is a dynamic inner universe for the individual unconscious. The self, as we have noted, is not a static category but a continual process of integration, what Jung calls individuation. In the whirling, neverending process of integration are the unconscious desires and aims as well as the conscious, societally conditioned goals. Jung's concept of persona is perceptive; it is widely appreciated even beyond his circle of adherents. The persona is the individual's front to the world, his mask. Indeed Jung's doctrine of the shadow, and of the anima/animus—the opposite self-image in the unconscious which maintains a kind of antiphonal relationship with the conscious self-image or persona, is based on valid observations of personality trends—both conscious and unconscious, as revealed in dreams and symbols. The woman in a man's dreams may represent his mother or sweetheart. But, even more deeply within his unconscious self-process, she represents himself, It is that self which biologically and psychologically is most neglected in his waking life. She also represents the archetypal woman of the racial unconscious. This latter construction may be rejected or held in suspended judgment. However, we are not compelled to discard Jung's suggestive insights as to the nature of the individual unconscious.

The clinical relevance of any theory of psychogenesis and of the ego is in the therapist's attempt to locate or explicate an emotional illness and to apply a remedy. Freudians, for example, may see an oral fixation in the alcoholic, as in the manic-depressive. Compulsion neurosis may stem from emotional traumata during the anal stage, which is a time of ritual for the child. Sadism, masochism, and obsessions to hoard, to grasp, to collect, revert to fixations during the anal period, say the orthodox. Oral sadism suggests the dental, or teething, phase of orality. This extends to verbal sadism, perhaps. An unresolved Oedipus complex may account for obsessive rebellion against authority. The fear of being humiliated and the surging hostility which accompanies it hark back to both the anal and the phallic—early Oedipal—stages.

Psychoanalysis describes the psyche as only partially developed, even when it is relatively healthy. Everyone's growth is somewhat stunted by fixations. A person may appear to be well-balanced, integrated, adjusted, until he is hit by some disturbing event which forces him back to a phase of his emotional development when the affected components were fixated on some object or solution which is the only one he knows that is appropriate for the kind of trauma he is again experiencing. We may liken the Freudian "component instincts"—and the history of their encounters—and the ego which develops by stages to an army, some of whose contingents have had to remain behind at various stations along the march. Setbacks mean retreat to places manned by friendly troops along the route.

The Freudian man can say: "I am all that I have met, all that I have incorporated and all to which I have become attached—all that I have cathected, all that I have taken into myself." Like the Gerasene demoniac he says, "My name is Legion; for we are many."

Such a reduction of the psyche to mechanistic systems of energy-seeking satisfaction by or against whatever objects happen to be in the way leads to a curious explanation even for such disciplines as psychology and medicine. The desire to discover the dynamics of the human unconscious, to spin psychoanalytic webs of theory in which to trap the impulses for closer examination, is a variant of infantile epistemophilia. This is a development by displacement of the infant's forbidden desires to see and to explore the bodies of his parents. His frustrated energy is harnessed to the socially acceptable exploration of one of the many disciplines being plied within the society. Thus in its most speculative moments psychoanalysis assays to explain a Plato, an Augustine, a Kant, and a Sigmund Freud.

Although some of his description may ever seem grotesque to many who read Freud on the genesis and the depths of mind, his work continues to be taken seriously. Some of its cogency is in the sheer power of his imagination. Some is in the unusual clarity with which he could express his theory. He makes it difficult for anyone to doubt that there is an intricate interrelation of the rational with the irrational in every man's psychology.

Otto Rank says that Freud goes further and tries the impossible, to present a rational account of what is essentially irrational. But Freud may have made a lasting contribution to our understanding of ourselves by insisting that the process of conscious thinking always be seen in relation to continuous somatic desiring and feeling. Who can dispute the assertion that human behavior proceeds somatically, even beyond the formative era of infancy? How incalculable is the determining power of the appetites, the nervous system, the vital organismic, biological selves of even the most soma-denying ascetics! We know, for instance, that the verbalized descriptions of mystical experience depend on the analogy of the biological satisfactions of hunger, thirst, muscular tension, warmth, and the desire for intimacy.

To Freud the basic organism—or id—knows not time. The Kantian categories are graspers by which the ego learns its milieu. Freud could agree with his arch opponent, Jung, that the past and the present are alike to the unconscious. A generation to the unconscious is as a day. It is the ego, the socialized or acculturated outgrowth of the id, which consciously anticipates and reminisces.

It is what suffers. This is certainly true if consciousness is a requisite for what is generally meant by suffering. The ego alone is conscious, although it is partially submerged in the unconscious. As we have noted earlier, psychotherapy is essentially ego therapy. The goal of therapy is to strengthen the ego in its control of the irrational id, as well as the irrational superego. The ego is the agency of reason, of conscious volition and of planning. It is the executive self, weak though it may be.

The so-called ego psychologists among contemporary Freudians are trying to maintain Freud's somatic psychology, while they elaborate the study of the ego. As we have pointed out, Freudian concentration on the ego seems to be assimilating insights presented by other schools such as Horney's and even Adler's.

In recent years the Freudian ego psychologist Erik H. Erikson has been reaching a wide audience. He is a man of parts, having maintained close ties with anthropologists and sociologists. From his youth he has had wide cultural interests, as have many of the theorists who have been attracted to the Freudian model. Freud's daughter, Anna, was Erikson's analyst and teacher. In 1960 he became Professor of Human Development at Harvard. In addition to numerous papers, he has written *Childhood and Society, Young Man Luther, Insight and Responsibility,* and *Gandhi's Truth.* In the psychoanalytic study of Luther, which is one of the best examples of the genre, he looks at the stages of life in Luther's biography.

Erikson presents a refined psychogenesis in an outline of eight stages, which are somewhat reminiscent of Sullivan's list. They are: (1) infancy: trust versus mistrust, (2) early childhood: autonomy versus shame and doubt, (3) play age: initiative versus guilt, (4) school age: industry versus inferiority, (5) adolescence: identity versus identity diffusion, (6) young adult: intimacy versus isolation, (7) adulthood: generativity versus self-absorption, and finally, (8) mature age: integrity versus disgust, despair. With the name of each stage there is the accompanying polarity which defines the nature of the crisis for each.

The identity crisis is the Oedipus situation. "Love for the maternal person who awakens his senses and his sensuality with her ministrations, and deep and angry rivalry with the male possessor of this maternal person" characterize the child at this stage.[6] This stage overlaps with others. It sets in before the stage of proficiency with some tool or tools, which, in *Young Man Luther,* marks the resolution of the identity crisis. With Luther, as with other religious and political reformers, says Erikson, the identity crisis is especially prolonged. The crisis can be tentatively resolved and then allowed to reappear. Perhaps in ego psychology we are witnessing a kind of integrity crisis for the genius of depth psychology. The Adlerian individual psychology with its emphasis on "life style," the Jungian emphasis on life energy and dynamic selfhood moving ever toward integration—"individuation," Horney's brilliant clinical descriptions of "neurotic trends" and conflicting "self images" (striving for identity), Sullivan's concept of the "waking self" within the "self dynamism," which is shaped by the process of interpersonal relations, Fromm's emphasis on the individual's quest for meaning in his own life, and Otto Rank's recognition of the necessity for the ego to implement the expression of the "self-validating irrational" in human nature, and his insistence on the ego as will—all these directions in the world of depth psychology outside the Freudian circle may possibly be assimilated by the ego psychology within it. At least we can say that all these emphases which we have cited seem to be in a considerable measure appropriate within the system of psychology which is set forth in the works of Erikson.

Of course, this is not to say that his thought includes all the elements within the systems of the theorists mentioned. Indeed much is to be gained by keeping the various theories separated, allowing for the many angles of vision upon our question.

In speaking of "ego integrity" Erikson says that there is no clear definition for it. But he ventures to name some of its constituents. It is the accumulated assurances that the ego itself prefers order to chaos and meaning to mere activity. He says that "ego strength" is measured relative to the strength of drives and

6. Erik H. Erikson, *Young Man Luther: A Study in Psychoanalysis and History* (New York: W. W. Norton & Co., Inc., 1958), p. 113.

trends which are at variance in the psyche-organism. Real strength is measured by its power to direct and control these. A so-called strong personality may actually be that of a relatively weak ego. That is, if the id and the superego energies have not been brought under control and assimilated by the executive, waking, prospective I of awareness.

Ego integrity is "a post-narcissistic love of the human ego—not the self—as an experience which conveys some world order and some spiritual sense, no matter how dearly paid for." In his venture into history and theology, with his psychoanalytic equipment, Erikson waxes eloquent, producing a kind of doxology to integrity:

> It is the acceptance of one's one and only life cycle as something that had to be and that, by necessity, permitted of no substitutions: it thus means a new, a different love of one's own parents. . . . Although aware of the relativity of all the various life styles which have given meaning to human striving, the possessor of integrity is ready to defend the dignity of his own life style against all physical and economic threats. For he knows that an individual life is the accidental coincidence of but one life cycle with but one segment of history; and that for him all human integrity stands or falls with the one style of integrity of which he partakes. The style of integrity developed by his culture or civilization thus becomes the 'patrimony of his soul,' the seal of his moral paternity of himself . . . Before this final solution, death loses its sting.[7]

Were Erikson to go on and say with Paul that the sting of death is sin, we would have explicit correlation of the hamartiology of depth psychology with that of Christian theology, perhaps. Certainly we do have something like a doctrine of sin and something like a doctrine of salvation in Erikson's thought. The tragic, if not the sinful, condition is the failure to surmount these crises; one or all of them: trust, will power, initiative, industry, identity, intimacy, generativity, and integrity. Integration is analogous to complete salvation and sanctification in traditional Christian doctrine. The ego of the ego integrity envisioned by Erikson is perhaps the optimum subject-self, or accountable I, to be found anywhere in psychoanalytic literature.

7. *Childhood and Society* (New York: W. W. Norton & Co., Inc., 1950), pp. 231–32. Erikson quotes himself in *Young Man Luther*, pp. 206–61.

The religious man—"homo religiosus"—says Erikson, is likely the victim and sometimes the hero of a life-long, chronic, integrity crisis. Because of only partially resolved infancy and childhood crises and a prolongation of the identity crisis, the religious man becomes older in one respect than his peers, his parents and teachers. Suddenly he focuses on what others take a lifetime to gain a mere inkling of perhaps, namely "the questions of how to escape corruption in living and how in death to give meaning to life." One thinks of the stories about the young Zarathustra, Vardhamana (Mahavira), Siddhartha Gautama (the Buddha), and Jesus—as a youth discussing weighty matters with the doctors. Erikson says, "The chosen young man extends the problem of his identity to the borders of existence in the known universe"; while others "bend all their efforts to adopt and fulfill the departmentalized identities which they find prepared in their communities.[8]

C. G. Jung would hardly encourage the hope that complete integration within the self is probable. Existence itself, fragmented, ambiguous, necessarily refractive, precludes any such perfection. Individuation is an unending process, in which the secret is to hold together the disparate, the polarities of light and darkness, good and evil, without ever expecting complete resolution.[9]

However, the description which Erikson draws of "ego integrity" may be a useful goal to set before the patient—the person. Perhaps it is more poetic and psychological than realistic. Nevertheless, a question remains as to whether the optimum "state of soul" is indeed that which Erikson describes.

Does the ego of "ego integrity" open sufficiently to what we may call the fourth dimension with which Christian theology, for instance, is concerned? The fourth dimension or fourth compass is that which transcends mere individual conscience, societal norms, and environmentally determined "conscience." Constructive, edifying love (agape) may not be readily characteristic of the self-contained person. True, we must not equate self-containedness

8. *Young Man Luther*, p. 262.
9. See *The Development of Personality*, Bollingen Series XX, Vol. 17 (New York: Bollingen Foundation, 1954), pp. 179, 196–97; and *Psychology and Alchemy* (*Ibid.* XX, 12), p. 208.

to Erikson's ego integrity. However, the question is relevant: What kind of person is a means of grace to others? Moreover, without *homo religiosus* and his never-quite-resolved integrity crisis, where could the prophetic element be in society? Of course we shall leave such questions open.

What is the nature of the I in "I am conscious"? Depth psychology helps us both to raise the question and to seek answers for it. Who, or what in a person, is the agency of responsible action? Who is it that knows good and evil?

In our story of the man-in-rage, in the first chapter, we confronted the difficulties in trying to focus the culpability even for an obviously outrageous offense. What in his confused world was accountable?

Our discussion of Freud's psychology, and of various schools' critical and corrective views, leads us to a choice between two faiths or working suppositions: (1) a commitment to the idea of determinism which practically denies that the waking self has any freedom or responsibility beyond those that are seen in the analogy of the flower—or weed—which tries to grow and to fulfill its destiny even in a patch of weeds, (2) a commitment to the idea of a significant area of free choice for the waking self—or ego—with the accompanying responsibility.

The logic of the Freud who posited a primal, victorious death instinct, seems to support the first position. Perhaps the logic of the early Freud, who taught the doctrine of libido as pleasure seeking and constrained only by reality as signalled by pain, gives precious little, if any, support to the second position. However, the spirit of Freud the therapist, ego psychologist, and social philosopher, and the genius of depth psychology in general throughout its various schools seem to favor the second faith.

If we continue to assume that there is an executive self which says I, which rationalizes even irrational behavior when pressed for a reason, which assumes responsibility, regardless of whether it should, then we are ready to examine the question of guilt and accountability.

3

Freedom and Responsibility:

Freud on Guilt Feelings

Once, in a debate with O. Hobart Mowrer, an eminent research psychologist, Albert Ellis, a New York psychotherapist who has by now gained some renown, argued that no human being should ever be blamed for anything he does. Nevertheless he agreed that "there is such a thing as human wrongdoing or immoral behavior." Before he granted this point, however, he described what he called "two elements in the sense of 'sin,' namely, (a) 'I have done the wrong thing and am responsible for doing it'; and (b) 'I am a blackguard, . . . a valueless person.' "[1] Mowrer has become well-known for his call for the use of guilt as an instrument in "the cure of souls" (psychotherapy).[2] The debate illustrates, to be sure, the confusion that abounds on such topics; rarely do the disputants really get together on the meaning of the terms they use; for example, "sin" and "guilt." In this particular exchange both men seemed to agree that therapy should not demolish one's "mature" sense of responsibility, to whatever extent such may exist. Dr. Ellis' objection seems to center on the second element which he described: the sense that "I am a blackguard, . . . a valueless person." This element conforms to what we shall discuss under the rubric "shame" rather than "guilt."

As we explore the nature of guilt feeling, we find just such complications as that which Ellis' statement illustrates. These include feelings of unworthiness, pervasive anxiety, and the danger of falling into despair, a phenomenon in itself. Then we are

1. Our reference is to a news release and transcripts published by the American Psychological Association (Washington, D.C., September 4, 1959).
2. O. H. Mowrer, "The Role of the Concept of Sin in Psychotherapy," in *The Journal of Counseling Psychology*, VII (1960), pp. 185–88, and his "'Sin' the Lesser of Two Evils," in *American Psychologist*, XV (1960), pp. 301–4.

puzzled still by the problem of how to interpret and to deal with that non-guilt-assuming kind of self-assertion which most anyone knows something about. What in a person voices the driving conviction, "Myself right or wrong!" Is it primary narcissism, is it an innate aggressiveness instinct, is it purposive libido, is it compensating energy which is trying to reverse an inner conviction of inferiority or "Myself wrong!" is it the executive self, the ego, perhaps in the service of irrational drives?

Of course, we are interested, also, in the question of good and evil, as well as the consciousness into which we have fallen. As we continue to explore, we shall look first at the question of the guilty conscience, the feeling that "I have done wrong."

In inquiring about the nature of guilt feelings we shall spend a chapter with Freud and then inquire of the others.

We begin with a homely incident. This is a domestic scene, a father-son episode. A two-year-old, on being reprimanded at the breakfast table, gets down from his high chair crying. He protests through tears, "Me good boy!" Who said he was not? Something in the event of correction itself says to him in effect, "You are a bad boy." This he cannot abide. So he bursts out for all the world to hear, "Me good boy!"[3]

Meanwhile his father's conscience hurts him. The fierceness of his reprimand has more than met the crime. He came to breakfast irritable. Now he sees himself as that artilleryman who brought down a canary with a cannon ball.

The inner pain continues as the father rides in to work. At his machine he finds himself coming back to the incident. All day long he cannot leave, emotionally, the breakfast table where he spoke in anger to his tiny son.

How is the troubled conscience quieted? Is not the problem how to satisfy it? The cry is for righting a wrong, for justification, if not of the deed, at least of the *I* who did it. The "mechanism" of rationalization is usually in frantic operation as the victim of guilt feelings tries to resume normal efficiency at his work.

---

3. Cf. a somewhat similar example related in Theodor Reik's *Confessions of An Analyst* (in the edition *The Search Within,* [New York: Farrar, Straus and Cudahy, 1956], pp. 231–33).

However, the satisfaction which guilt feelings seek is not to be made in a merely fictional way. True, if given their way, they would turn the clock back—indeed, they do in fantasy, compulsively, repetitively—and reseat the man at the breakfast table, run the scene again, correcting the reprimand. The child would be addressed in a quiet, loving manner. Then and only then could the father feel truly "justified" in the sense of being made "righteous" in the situation. The portrait of his unhappy infant son persists before his mind's eye. "If only I had not been so harsh! If only I could go back and do it right!" Regret in some situations may even turn into remorse.

Obviously the father cannot go back to the event and undo it. What then can he do? He will try to be especially good to the boy when he goes home tonight. He will make a kind of reparation, a restitution, hence, an "expiation." The making of restitution, while never a perfect "justification," is as near as one can come to it on his own.

In the evening when the father sees his son again and in his own way does the work of reparation, thus showing his son that he does love him—and thus probably reassuring the small boy that he is accepted by his father as "good" instead of "bad," he is rewarded by the son's affection—tantamount to forgiveness. The son is accepting him as the "good" father. How like the child's spontaneous outburst of the morning, "Me good boy," is the father's work of reparation! It seems to express, "I am a good father." In his psyche the image of his injured son is close to his own damaged self-image.[4] The son's accepting him as the good father is the forgiveness sought even as the father's accepting, attentive demonstration to the son is the forgiveness or reassurance which is desired by the child, at least in the moment of injury. To be sure, the day's soothing events (possibly soothing—there could have been a pile-up of negative experiences for the child) may have done much of the job by the time father gets home. How-

4. See such interesting, yet typical, Freudian discussions as Ernest Jones' "The Significance of the Grandfather for the Fate of the Individual," and "The Phantasy of the Reversal of Generations," reprinted in Jones' *Papers on Psycho-Analysis*, 4th ed., Chap. 27 and 28 (London: Bailliere, Tindall and Cox, 1938), pp. 519–24, 525–30.

ever, within the mind of the father the work of reconciliation is waiting to be done.

As an armchair anthropologist, Sigmund Freud came to regard guilt as universal, specifically Oedipal guilt. We may regret that he spelled out the nature of guilt in so reductionistic a manner, but we can hardly appreciate his thought on the subject without following him about within the Oedipal frame of reference. First he simply speculated, but then, even before moving on to another essay, he was building theory upon his speculation, and he had a habit of using the whole bit—speculative foundation and imaginative superstructure—in subsequent essays as a necessary part of their thesis, indeed as building blocks or as a corner structure of his expanding walled city. Not only was parricide—or parricidal fantasy—the "sin" of the individual, but it was the primordial guilt of the whole human race. And, as in the case of the individual, it is because of incestuous love for the mother, the father's woman (primordially, the tyrant's women).

In *Totem and Taboo* (1914), Freud likens the totem sacrifice and meal, as described by W. Robertson Smith in *The Religion of the Semites* (1889), to the Christian celebration of Communion and the theology implicit in it. Also, he relates the accompanying taboo, a concept from which he freely but somewhat carefully generalizes an elaborate web, directly to Christian ethics. Of course Christianity is not the only one invited to this web. To Freud, all religion and all other "compulsion neuroses" are directly related to the primitive drama however it may be re-enacted in customs of "totem and taboo." Superstition is a vestige of primitive taboo. From primordial taboo were derived both our sense of the sacred and our sense of the forbidden and the unclean.

The basic taboo, says Freud, is against incest with the mother, or father's wife. All other taboos stem from this one. The origin of the taboo was the primal father's own will. Incest is integrally related to murder in the racial, as well as the individual, psyche! Already Freud has spoken of the human organism's hostility to culture because of the pressure it exerts against the id, and "the instinctual renunciations that it demands." If its prohibitions were removed, then one—the Freudian protagonist is the male—could choose any woman he wanted and kill without hesitation, any rival; he could take whatever he wanted of another man's possessions. "What a succession of delights life would be" but for the fact that one would find that everyone else is trying to exercise the same liberty.[5]

In primordial society, therefore, says Freud, only one person could have such rights. He was the primordial tyrant, who of course must have wanted the males under him to respect the cultural commandment: Thou shalt not kill. Hence, the first taboos were against incest and against murder of the possessor of the women. Apparently, to the imagination of Freud, the boys could not take it any longer. There was incest crisis and murder. The incest problem in the dawn of culture, along with the repetition of such a crisis in the psychogenesis of every individual who develops beyond the phallic stage, accounts for the prevalent association of "sin" with sexual offenses and desires.

Furthermore, the primitive desire to commit incest, essentially an offense against the tyrant father, is equivalent to parricide, since its fulfillment would require the removal of the father-chief. Freud sees, not only in the behavior of other mammals, but in Hebrew, Greek, and Persian myths, and in the practice of taboo and totem ritual in primitive societies, a compelling witness to an early murder of the father of the race and the emergence of a society of brothers. The original sin was murder of the father. It was followed immediately by the fear of retribution. The father image could not be killed. It remained and has remained to haunt the imagination of the sons. In order to ward off the threat of reprisals, the sons consolidated their fraternity and formed a father-worshipping cult in an attempt to appease him, to undo the murder. The father was identified with a certain animal, the totem animal, after which the tribe was likely named. By projection the image was invested with deity.

5. Freud seems to assume a social contract theory of society, at least with respect to the prior "state of nature." See *Civilization and Its Discontents* in *Complete Psychological Works*, trans. Joan Riviere, Vol. 21 (London: Hogarth, 1930), p. 95. He uses *Totem and Taboo* both in that work and in his polemic against religion in *The Future of An Illusion* (1927), and in his *Moses and Monotheism* (1939).

Henceforth the father image was regarded with ambivalence: (1) reverence and even tenderness, and (2) the old hatred of the domineering, selfish, restrictive tyrant. The deified figure is approached with guilt-conditioned emotions and also with renewed hatred. Human and animal sacrifice have served a dual purpose: re-enactment of the murder and retributive execution of one of the sons or a substitute for him. The mortally offended tribal father-god is ever in pursuit of his parricidal sons.

"Of course these cannibalistic savages ate their victim." Thus, they identified with the father by incorporating him. Each man thereby acquired part of the father's strength. The totem feast, which Freud surmised was perhaps the first celebration, would be the compulsive repetition of the murder and eating of the father, the sin with which so many things began, including the institutions of society, ethics, and religion.[6]

The brothers' crime was something of a failure. But, Freud says, failure is more conducive to moral reaction than success. The suppressed tenderness emerged in the form of remorse, which expressed itself as conscious guilt feeling. How did they try to make reparation, to undo their deed? Why, by making it a crime to commit murder and by renouncing the fruits of their conquest, the father's women. Thus out of the primal guilt of parricide they created the two taboos against murder and incest, the two sources of morality and religion according to Freud.

Incest prohibition had another strong support, besides the desire to appease the dead father. "Sexual need does not unite men; it separates them." Perhaps some advance in culture such as a new weapon had given the brothers a temporary feeling of superiority. In the aftermath when they find that they are each other's rivals they somehow manage to live together by introducing enforceable laws.

In *Moses and Monotheism*, Freud's last book, the notion of parricide is still very much on the aging writer's mind. He assumes, following a statement once made—and possibly later effectively

6. *Totem and Taboo*, trans. James Strachey (New York: W. W. Norton & Co., Inc., 1952), pp. 141–42.

retracted—by Ernst Sellin,[7] that Moses was murdered by the Hebrews in the wilderness.

Freud asks himself why the idea of monotheism made such a deep impression on his own people and why they have adhered to it so tenaciously. He thinks the answer is in the repetition of the primal murder. They did it again! "It was a case of acting instead of remembering, something which often happens during analytic work with neurotics." They actually used the doctrine of the murdered Moses, namely, monotheism, as a means of denying their guilt. Later, Paul of Tarsus picked up the psychological thread. Says Freud, "It can scarcely be chance that the violent death of another great man should become the starting point for the creation of a new religion by Paul." He and other adherents in Judea fit the new figure to the paradigm: son of God, Messiah, a kind of Moses, to whom, later, was given some of the "childhood history that had been attached to Moses."[8]

The two religions are different in that the Jewish expression of monotheism amounts to a denial—a repression—of parricidal guilt, a self-justification, while the Christian faith looks back to the death of the "Son of God" as the enduring sacrifice which appeased the Father by giving life for life. The Son bore the guilt of the whole world of mankind. Freud knew what it was to be a Jew in what he regarded as a somewhat antisemitic culture, Viennese. As a Jew he witnessed the encroaching hysteria of Hitlerism, and he wrote, toward the end of his eighty-two years:

> The poor Jewish people, who with its usual stiff-necked obduracy continue to deny the murder of their "father," has dearly expiated this in the course of centuries. Over and over again they heard the reproach: you killed our God. And this reproach is true, if rightly interpreted. It says, in reference to the history of religion: you

7. Sellin, *Mose und seine Bedeutung* (Leipzig: A. Deichertsche Verlagsbuchhandlung, 1922). See Ernest Jones' account in *The Life and Work of Sigmund Freud*, Vol. 3 (London: Hogarth, 1953), pp. 363–74. Freud made much of the possible link between Moses and the Amarna revolution and the short-lived religion of Akhenaten, a theory which is much disputed, see Theophile James Meek, *Hebrew Origins* (New York: Harper & Row, 1960), pp. 184–228.

8. *Moses and Monotheism*, trans. Katherine Jones (New York: Alfred A. Knopf, 1939), pp. 144–45.

won't *admit* that you murdered God (the archetype of God, the primaeval Father and his reincarnations). Something should be added, namely: "It is true, we did the same thing, but we *admitted* it, and since then we have been purified.[9]

Freud's Moses was an Egyptian not a Jew. Paul's Jesus, Freud recognized, was a Jew. Thus we have the curious inversion: the "successful" gentile religion re-enacting its ambivalence toward the Jewish figure Jesus, as father and brother deity and the unsuccessful, perennially persecuted, Jewish religion, which has repressed its hatred of its non-Jew father, Moses, whom it consciously regards with reverence.

The Christianity which Freud had in mind is principally its expression in Roman Catholicism, as he saw it in the surrounding culture where he spent most of his life. The Christianity which he observed seemed, to him, to regard sexual desire as evil in itself in insisting on the celibacy of the priesthood and in defining sin as originating in sexual lust. In his last writings, Freud reaffirmed his convictions expounded a generation earlier in *Totem and Taboo* (and before he introduced the notion of a death instinct and "guilt" as derivative from it). In that book Freud said that the original sin, according to Christianity, is really murder of a primal father—deicide. He inferred from the sacrifice of the Mass and the accompanying doctrine about redemption through the death of Christ on the cross, that "if this sacrifice of a life brought about atonement with God the Father, the crime to be expiated can only have been the murder of the father."[10]

In a footnote to the sentence preceding the one quoted, he anticipated a theory of psychic economics which he was to develop in his paper, "Mourning and Melancholia" (1917). The footnote says, "We find that impulses to suicide in a neurotic turn out regularly to be self-punishments for wishes for someone else's death." Freud's reasoning seemed to be bound by a conviction that the psyche's logic is that the crime must fit the punishment. Hence, if doctrine, symbol, or myth say death, then it must be punishment for parricide. Perhaps, had Freud already derived his

9. *Ibid.*, p. 145. Cf. at p. 215.
10. *Totem and Taboo,* p. 154.

theory of a destructiveness instinct by the time he began this line of speculation, then he may have abandoned the project or else shaped it quite differently. True, the "repetition compulsion" he saw in religious ritual and in the behavior of various patients (especially World War I shell-shock victims) helped lead him to the notion of a death instinct. Moreover, he, when writing *Civilization and Its Discontents* (1929), wished to restrict the origin and sense of guilt to the aggressive (death) instincts.[11]

We have reviewed Freud's theologonic mythology not at all because we think it is true or in any sense established in the social scientific community. Certainly his theories can be questioned at many points and often refuted outright. However, like speculative philosophy and some theology Freud's speculations in the study of anthropology and religion have had wide influence. In the minds of some his speculations have even been confused with his science. Moreover as we noted before, he tended to carry over his doctrines from one context into another; hence, once he had posited racial guilt (1913) he presupposed it then in his clinical work.[12]

Society, as well as the individual, tries by ritual to win freedom from the fear in guilt. According to Freud, both tend to re-enact their sins and achieve a kind of temporary feeling of atonement. "Justification" comes by "keeping the feast," whether in the observance of the communal sacrament or in private act of fantasy.

In the individual, *at-one-ness* with the parental images is effected by psychic incorporation, or introjection. The introjected disapproving, threatening images form the nucleus for the I which transcends, often uncontrollably, the I which is supposed to be in rational control. The introjected norms of society are the inner moral law, the conscience. Much of any individual's behavior can be described as his attempt to satisfy his inner, introjected critic.

Freud produces on large canvas his portrait of the individual. To be sure, it is impressionistic, both Freudian and impressionistic.

---

11. *Complete Psychological Works*, Vol. 21, pp. 130–31, text and note.
12. See for example, his case study in 1918, "From the History of an Infantile Neurosis," in *Complete Psychological Works*, Vol. 17, pp. 3–137. Cf. Freud's appraisal of Otto Rank's theory of *Geburtstrauma*, *infra*.

Guilt feeling may become repressed, like any other emotion, and seethe within the unconscious, even when the ego may have given up the attempt to make restitution. The economics of the psyche will see to it that the irrational and unconscious will somehow get expressed. Repressed guilt may come through as acute attacks of anxiety, or, worse, a sudden explosive, perhaps destructive, bursting forth of the damned-up energy. Ego mechanisms of displacement, sublimation, and projection may be used for the control of repressed guilt feeling and its frequent companion, hostility. Freud utilized these concepts of mental mechanisms in explaining the origin of religion and culture. Compulsion neurosis is a way of controlling the tension between inner drives and the outside reality. By compulsive, substitutive behavior the individual and the society are held together, by corporate expression in alternation, both of the sin and of the justification, both the offense-hostility and the resolution of guilt feelings.

In spite of the restrictive frame of reference in which we find Freud's doctrine of sin and guilt, we see a perceptive delineation of the components of guilt feeling. It is composed of (1) the fear of being destroyed, of self-loss, of mutilation, of retaliation by the one offended, (2) the fear of object-loss; that is, the loss of the loved image of the person-object offended, and (3) compulsion, often oppressive and sadistic toward the ego; as "repetition compulsion" in re-enacting the offense it may be interpreted as a form of continuing hostility. Also, in compulsion, there is likely to be the dynamic fearfulness, which Melanie Klein recognizes, of one's own potential for destructive aggressiveness. Guilt, even for Freud, presupposes love, although it is eros, sometimes depicted as the force which effects libidinal cathexis of objects. Guilt feelings acknowledge the claims of a relationship which has been violated. Guilt is a confluence of other feelings or emotions: specifically, love, fear, and hostility.[13] If Suttie and others are right in deriving hatred from fear of the loss of love, the simple definition of guilt as "fear of the consequences" may not be too far from the mark. The consequences are, prototypically, the loss of the

13. See, for instance, *Civilization and Its Discontents*, pp. 106–7.

love on which one depends for his life, or for what he deems his life.

The authority that finds out, hence, the authority which is feared, before whom one has what we call a bad conscience, is the villain superego itself. For instance, if we look at the "relatively strict and vigilant conscience" which is "the very sign of a virtuous man," what do we find beneath the surface? "Though saints may proclaim themselves sinners, they are not so wrong, in view of the temptations of instinctual gratifications to which they are peculiarly liable—since temptations do but increase under constant privation."[14]

Renunciation will not do the trick. Here is a "great disadvantage economically" in the erection of this agency within the psyche. The superego, or, loosely, the conscience, is always there to condemn the person for even having the desire. Hence, in his flight from the frown of external authority, man has landed under the relentless glare of an entrenched persecutor-for-righteousness-sake in residence. "In the beginning conscience (more correctly, the anxiety which later became conscience) was the cause" of the renunciation of instinctual desire. But, alas, instead of elation, misery is compounded. "Every renunciation . . . becomes a dynamic fount of conscience; every fresh abandonment of gratification increases its severity and intolerance.[15]

14. *Ibid.,* p. 109.
15. *Ibid.,* pp. 112, 113–14.

4

Freedom and Responsibility:

Others on Guilt Feelings

Leaving the Freudian world, we may welcome the comparatively simple *de facto* definitions of guilt which Harry Stack Sullivan provides. First, he distinguishes "guilt" from what he calls "sublimational or rationalistic" guilt, which he regards merely as a defense against some other distress. Sullivan's genuine guilt feeling is a gnawing, sleep-disturbing kind of awareness of having committed an offense against one's own "personality organization," of having committed an actual "crime in an interpersonal sense," an injury felt by the "self-dynamism." The waking, conscious active person is the sum of all his interpersonal relationships. Guilt is the awareness that one has actually done something or failed to do something and thus threatened the security of these relationships in their external and internalized form. Such guilt feeling must be dealt with in terms of the actual offense. Good therapy cannot gloss over its importance.[1]

True, the Freudians also have recognized a "pseudo-guilt" (the term Sullivan likes to use) from which they have distinguished a more "authentic" guilt. When it is focused on trivial matters, "guilt feeling" is a symptom of a deeper distress and need. It is what Sullivan calls rationalistic guilt—or sublimational. Hortatory ethics and religion, programs of careful indoctrination, political, confessional, social, and cultural, these often try to focus guilt feelings. It can be used in erecting an elaborate, sometimes deceptive, superstructure in society which can function as an easily available—indeed often intrusive—external "conscience" for the individual and the group. If this artificial authority—say, the

1. *Clinical Studies in Psychiatry* (New York: W. W. Norton & Co., Inc., 1956), pp. 112–15. Cf. Karen Horney, *The Neurotic Personality of Our Time* (New York: W. W. Norton & Co., Inc., 1937), p. 257.

Party, the Church, the Union, the Club, the Office—decrees a course of action as "right," then the responsive conscience is so informed. Such a use of the human capacity for guilt feeling is degrading and guilty of an offense against humanity, perhaps more often than not. A person can be conditioned to feel or to assume guilt for a variety of things and move farther and farther away from the opportunity to live responsibly in community as a person in authentic relationship with other persons. He may be conditioned to feel, or at least to assume, guilt for, and to spend himself on, trifles. In both collective and private rituals he can act out his need for reconciliation, purification, and—harking back to Freud, again—the renewal of aggression. "Conscience" itself may become a blinder. By indulging this conscience a person may be defending himself against the fear of becoming aware of his true self, his realistic limitations, and his actual situation.

Perhaps no depth psychologist who treats this phenomenon of guilt feeling addresses it simply as therapist. Indeed, the very process of therapy implies a certain faith and what theologians might be inclined to call a soteriological commitment. It is true, Freud pressed his speculative inquiry all the way to a primal theology with an original racial guilt occurring over incest and parricide. Sullivan speaks of "crime in an interpersonal sense." To be sure, he limits the range of his concern with the question of guilt. The right is whatever harmony is possible for this patient's —this person's—interpersonal relationships.

Although most therapists would aim at getting the client relatively free of any persisting feelings that bother him, most would regard an apparent absence of the capacity for conscious guilt feeling as hardly normal. Freudians would see it as a sure mark of immaturity.[2]

Karen Horney has undertaken to elucidate the nature of pathological guilt in its more accessible manifestations. In describing the person, she uses the phrase "personality structure." In this choice of words, perhaps the influence of Karl Abraham persists. As we recall, he shares the honors with Freud in outlining the

2. By "immaturity" they mean a pre-Oedipal "character type."

study of character, following the stages of libido-cathexis: oral, anal, phallic, (latent), and genital. In time, Horney tended to leave the somatic (and "organ specific") frame of reference off stage or at most as but a part of the setting. The resultant personality structure, which is quite like Alfred Adler's concept of "life style," became the focus of the drama. In her clinical work she seems to have rather effectively used whatever she felt she needed from the old Freudian kit. However, she anticipated Freudian ego-psychology—of course much of her work paralleled the development of this movement within the Freudian circle. Her reasoning was that since psychotherapy is "ego" therapy, why not focus on the personality structure as one finds it and enlist it in the conscious work of therapy? Here we see Adler's point on which he defected years before Freud got around to such a thesis as *The Ego and the Id* (1923).

According to Horney, in the neurotic (and many if not most of us can qualify) the "actual self" tries more or less futilely to rescue "the urge to grow" from the distorting mold which society forces upon it, and to turn it into its "natural" direction. She assumes that this potential real self is naturally the right one for the individual. His fall into sin is his being squeezed into a societally determined mold.[3] The sad part is that he feels guilty for resisting such artificial selfhood and for any failure to satisfy its demands. Hence the conscience itself is distorted, wrong, in urgent need of salvation, of reconstruction. The most far-reaching offense of all is that which is committed by society and especially by those who of necessity shape the lives of others, when they inculcate norms and ideals which are unrealistic, if not irresponsible. True, even society's offense against its members is often unwitting, blind. Yet, the most guilt-ridden person may in fact be the most sinned against.

As Erikson says, in his study of Luther:

> The most deadly of all possible sins is the mutilation of a child's spirit; for such mutilation undercuts the life principle of trust, without which every human act, may it feel ever so good, and seem

---

3. Cf. Rom. 12:2 (J. B. Phillips' translation points the parallel).

ever so right, is prone to perversion by destructive forms of conscientiousness.[4]

Karen Horney agrees with Freud that guilt is produced by fear. But she disagrees with his elaborated theory and with his concept of a nuclear inner agency of guilt in the superego. She tries to distinguish between what she calls "normal moral strivings" and the "tyranny of the should."[5] Perhaps her best contribution to the subject is her lively description of this tyranny. She scores Freudian theory for adopting the common view that the inner dictates are the inner construct of "morality in general." Commands for moral perfection cannot be separated from those, just as insistent, that argue no moral aim, such as for example, unconscious arrogance's pressure that may say, "I should always get the better of others." "I should be able to paint without laborious training and working." "I should be able to get away with anything." To disobey the shoulds is to feel guilt, as fear of the consequences. Guilt is basically anxiety. One's security is threatened, his overall satisfactions are apt to be cut off.

These coercive forces, the shoulds, whose real nature is never clearly discerned by the person who is enslaved by them, receive various patterns of obedience. Horney describes these according to the types of personality organization she has noted in her patients. They are: (1) the expansive types, who are bent on mastery at all costs, (2) the self-effacing types, (3) the resigned types, to whom the idea of freedom has special appeal, who rebel actively or passively against all demands upon them, and (4) the alternating types who vacillate between self-castigating goodness and a wild protest against any standards, constantly shuttling between "I should" and "No, I won't."[6]

Internal conflicts, derived formally from early environmental pressures may appear as external social conflicts. The feeling of guilt is but a symptom of a deeper emotion, the fear of rejection,

4. *Young Man Luther* (New York: W. W. Norton & Co., Inc., 1958), p. 70.
5. *Neurosis and Human Growth* (New York: W. W. Norton & Co., Inc., 1950), p. 73.
6. *Ibid.,* pp. 76–78.

of separation, of the return by one's action to an intolerable basic anxiety which is due to the earliest trauma and pattern of separation.

Ian Suttie developed his theoretical psychology from his own keen observation and research but *vis-à-vis* the Freudian theories. Primal matriarchal religions reflect Laius and Cain-type guilt and the offering up of innocent Oedipal-infant and Abel-sibling victims is at base simply the frightened human organism's trying to maintain or to regain security and love from the primal mother.

With the increasing recognition of the formative effect of mother images, both good and bad, guilt feelings are now described not simply with reference to ambivalence toward the father figure. Fear of the bad mother and loss of the good mother may indeed be something more than a modification of underlying feelings about the primal father. In the spirit of the critique offered by Suttie, depth psychology is rediscovering the matriarchal springs of even a patriarchal culture. Woman is not, as for the early Freud, merely or even predominantly a sexual object, nor is she to be defined in psychological theory by the image she holds in the mind of the male theorist.[7]

Suttie's portrait of the infant in his dilemma during the crisis of psychic weaning suggests that guilt feelings occur in some such manner as this: "If I do not love her then she will increasingly refuse to let me share with him (the sibling) in her nurturing love and care." The child cannot endure such fear. Yet he finds it difficult to control his rageful way of bidding for her love, his Abel-murdering way of trying to get back into his mother's good graces. Rage is self-defeating. Every instance of its failure causes fresh regret. He blames himself for the loss of the mother's cherishing love, especially when this seems to occur directly as the result of his censured behavior.

The child is faced with the problem of learning the riddle of psychic weaning. His problem is to understand and to adjust to

7. Cf. Freud, himself, correlating the mother image with "mother earth" and with "death" in "The Theme of the Three Caskets," (1913) in *Collected Papers*, Vol. 4 (London: Hogarth, 1956), pp. 244–56. Also, we recall, the primal guilt is over the possession of the mother.

the calamity which it seems to be. His sources are limited as he tries to work out a solution. Obviously he needs all the help his mother and the nurturing, loving environment can give him. "If only I had not done this or that then she would have taken me up and loved me. Something is wrong about me." How else can the impoverished self of the infant account for his change of status with the mother?

Good and evil are learned in this crisis of psychic weaning. Good and evil must be my good and evil. The infant lives in an undifferentiated world. Even the mother image is merged with the mothering image of the father and of other significant persons. "I and my mother are one." There is no I—no me—apart from her. This symbiotic union is broken, and society is born anew. The infant is forced to differentiate, to conceive of life in terms of "*you* and *I*." This is painful. The I retains mother images; indeed they are its portrait of itself. He experiences the mother increasingly not simply as the warm, nurturing, loving influences of his world, but as a complex image. The mother of reality is not simply love and adoration of him. She has other interests as well. He can either invest her with the predominantly good images he has of her as she was experienced before psychic weaning seemed to begin, or he can invest her with the predominantly bad ones. Hence, the primal conscience is shaped according to the infant's reflected pattern of what mother likes and what she does not like.

The more he thinks of his real mother as good, the more he will look for the evil—the cause of his dissatisfactions—within himself. The more he thinks of his real mother—and mother surrogates—as bad and denying toward him, the more he will look for the good within himself, where he has retained the good mother image.[8]

Regardless of the explanation, however, evil is subject to two definitions; it may be a force outside the self or a force inside. Although in everyone it is both "from the outside world" and "from within," there is considerable variety in the patterns of combination. The individual's particular way of defining evil may

8. Our construction here is supported by *The Origins of Love and Hate* (London: Kegan Paul, 1935), pp. 38–57; 61–67; 129–32; and *passim*.

well be one of the indices by which we distinguish temperament.[9]

If the outside world seems so hostile that no effective good mother image is internalized, the individual so deprived even of minimal loving care may be doomed to a hate-ridden, enemy-collecting existence, with rage as his way of life, because hostility more than love has been the order of the day from his beginning. In him guilt feeling will be almost entirely lacking because he has known so little love. He has never achieved enough trustfulness to be able to experience the much more complex emotion of guilt feeling.

Nowadays, especially, this construction of the theories relative to love and guilt feeling represents something of a consensus except perhaps among the dualistic Freudians. Yet even among them the theory persists that the only antidote to hostility is love.[10] "Fantasy is the mental corrollary to the instincts (Susan Isaacs). Like the instincts, fantasy operates from the onset. . . . The building up of a world of good and bad internal objects leads to internal persecution as well as to internal riches." The theory says, perhaps to astound us—unless we are used to reading long passages by Klein and Isaacs: "The internalized objects felt by the young infant have a life of their own. Persecution, suspicion, trust, and confidence result from their interaction."[11]

Michael Balint, a Freudian who reflects also the influence of the early master among the practicing analysts, Sandor Ferenczi, of Budapest, calls for a re-examination of the status of the "death instinct." True to the genius of Ferenczi, who, incidentally, was also the first teacher of Melanie Klein, and who had considerable

---

9. Cf. Jung's *Psychology of Types,* trans. H. Godwin Baynes (New York: Harcourt, Brace, 1923). His terms are now a part of the language: "introvert," "extrovert," and "ambivert." The more introverted person, according to Jung, is likely to be one whose early experience of the outside world was such that he soon tended to look—for the good—within; he was thrown back upon himself. Cf. Freud's theories of narcissism, *infra,* and Jean Piaget's numerous studies which use a similar insight.

10. For instance, see Melanie Klein and Joan Riviere, *Love, Hate, and Reparation* (London: Hogarth, 1937).

11. W. Hoffer's abstract of "The Mutual Influences in the Development of Ego and Id—Discussants," *The Psychoanalytic Study of the Child,* VII, in *The International Journal of Psycho-Analysis,* XXXIV (1953), p. 278.

influence on Suttie as well, Balint says that love is primary, even as the classical theory had it that erotic libido was primary. "Hate is a measure of inequality between object and subject; the smaller the inequality, the more mature the subject, the less is his need for hate."[12]

Separation is cardinal in the doctrines of Horney, Fromm, Sullivan, Suttie, and Otto Rank. Guilt feelings include the fear of another separation, from the loved object or constellation of objects: mother, father, and the objectified self. The fear of separation also includes the fear of pain and the fears which Melanie Klein emphasized, the fears of mutilation and extinction.[13] Certainly, Freud's mythical "history" of the fall of man and his theory of the genesis of the individual ego, feature separation: from the mother, the primordial tyrant's women, from the father, from the post-parricidal quarry; from the brothers—siblings; from the deified father.

We have seen how basic in Freud's thought is the concept of guilt. It is, if anything, even more developed and functional in the rather involved and ponderously articulated thought of his brilliant erstwhile disciple Otto Rank.

Freud took a special interest in young Rank while he was attending a technical school in Vienna. He saw marked perceptiveness in him and helped him financially. Rank graduated from the University of Vienna, where he specialized in social studies and philosophy. He was considered the intellectual giant among the apostles after the defection of Jung. He became one of the two lay analysts of the inner circle, the other being Hans Sachs. His contributions to the journals were meant largely to relate psychoanalysis to cultural and anthropological studies. He was the editor of *Imago,* the journal devoted to such interests, and was on the editorial staff of the *International Journal of Psycho-Analysis.*

---

12. M. Balint, "On Love and Hate," *Ibid.,* XXXIII (1952), pp. 355–62, at p. 359.
13. *The Psycho-Analysis of Children,* trans. Alix Strachey (London: Leonard and Virginia Woolf at Hogarth Press, 1932), pp. 184–85; *Developments in Psycho-Analysis,* ed. Joan Riviere (London: Hogarth, 1952), pp. 276, 278–79; and elsewhere.

However, by 1925, Rank, like his predecessors in 1911-13: Adler, Jung, and Wilhelm Stekel, was the center of controversy within the movement. The final break with the master himself was delayed until early in 1926. Both Freud and Rank died in 1939. Arch-Freudians like Ernest Jones have of course analyzed Rank's growing independence and his "defection" as Oedipal. Freud had taken a paternal interest in him, and Rank had been among his closest associates for over a decade. No doubt Suttie could give a "Laius" interpretation of the conflict. However, regardless of how it may be subject to clinical comment, the controversy may be bracketed for our purposes so that Rank as a theorist may be scrutinized. In any case, many outside the circle of Freudian solidarity have looked on Rank as a creative new theorist whose work should be considered in its own right. Before long his so-called will-therapy developed into something of a school on its own. He was striking out in directions, certain of which now, with the ego-psychologists like Erikson, can be regarded as "orthodox."

In 1923, Rank and Ferenczi published *The Development of Psychoanalysis*,[14] which along with Rank's "far more disturbing book"—according to Jones, *The Trauma of Birth,* published at about the same time, was the occasion for the storm.

Freud said the latter book was the "incomparably more interesting" one. He regarded it as "highly significant." At first, he said, "It has given me much to think about" and "I have not yet come to a definitive judgment about it."

We have long been familiar with womb phantasies and recognized their importance, but in the prominence Rank has given them they achieve a far higher significance and reveal in a flash the biological background of the Oedipus complex. To repeat it in my own language: some instinct must be associated with the birth trauma which aims at restoring the previous existence. One might call it the instinctual need for happiness (*Gluckstrieb*), understanding there that the concept "happiness" is mostly used in an erotic sense, Rank now goes further than psychopathology and shows how men alter the outer world in the service of this instinct, whereas

14. New York: Nervous and Mental Disease Publishing Co.

neurotics save themselves this trouble by taking the short cut of phantasying a return to the womb.

Then Freud suggests a construction which gives a clue to the boundaries which he has already set for the dispute. "If one adds to Rank's conception the one of Ferenczi, that a man can be represented by his genital, then for the first time we get a derivation of the normal sexual instinct which falls into place with our conception of the world."

Freud chose at first to keep the matter open for discussion, although he noted Rank's divergence from his own views. "I derived the barrier against incest from the primordial history of the human family, and thus saw the actual father the real obstacle, which erects the barrier against incest anew.[15]

It is important for us to note the intellectual issue which Freud identified in his first letter about the Rank book. He says that Rank "refuses to consider phylogenesis"! He gives him credit for at least this much adherence to the doctrine once delivered: "The birth anxiety is, it is true, transferred to the father," but according to Rank "alas!—he is only a pretext for it." In other words, Rank is suggesting that the primal anxiety is in the disturbance which the human organism experiences during the process of being born. The dual heresy is in the implied denial of (1) a racially inherited taboo against incest and (2) the absolute primacy of the father— both phylogenetically and psychogenetically—as the one to be feared, murdered (if only in fantasy) and appeased.

In this statement we can see the line taken by Freud's mounting disapproval of his disciple's thought. It was later elaborated in *Hemmung, Symptom und Angst*.[16] We see also another illustration of the way Freud linked his anthropological speculations with his psychology and how seriously he regarded the combination.

In August 1924, Freud wrote to Ferenczi, during one of the crises in his relationship with Rank: "I simply don't understand

15. The quotations are from a letter from Freud, February 15, 1924, to members of the central committee, in Jones', *The Life and Work of Sigmund Freud*, Vol. 3 (London: Hogarth, 1953), pp. 59–63, at pp. 61–62.

16. The English title is *Inhibitions, Symptoms, and Anxiety*, trans. Alix Strachey (London: Hogarth, 1926) or *The Problem of Anxiety*, trans. H. A. Bunker (New York: W. W. Norton & Co., Inc., 1936–   ).

Rank any longer. Can you do anything to enlighten me? . . . Which is the real Rank, the one I have known for fifteen years or the one Jones has been showing me in the past few years?" The sorrowing elder describes the Rank he once knew: "someone who was affectionately concerned, always ready to do any service." Had he been free to think his own thoughts? "He was," says Freud, "just as ready to receive new suggestions as he was uninhibited in the working out of his own ideas." Formerly, he "always took my side in a quarrel and, as I believed, without any inner compulsion to make him do so."[17]

Rank moved to Paris, later to the United States, where he gained a considerable following.[18] Ira Progoff regards Rank's *Psychology and the Soul,* which was written during 1929 and 1930, as an important statement of a system of thought which perceptively interprets human nature and culture with a good sense of history.[19] However, the book, like Suttie's, is difficult in form and style. Rank attempts to go "beyond psychology" by moving beyond what he considers the futile attempt to rationalize what is in its very essence irrational—beyond the grasp of reason. In Rank the irrational is a positive category. It cannot be gathered up into a "reasonal" form. Mental processes are mysterious, beyond our probing. Freud violates the mystery, the essentially "spiritual." Rank does not treat the terms "irrational" and "spiritual" as synonyms. The "spiritual" should have primacy over both the irrational and the rational. Its manifestation in the psyche is the "will to believe." He at times speaks of this "third principle" as the "will to immortality." It moves beyond individuality. The artist-life is the proper condition of health for the individual as for the society.

17. Jones, *Life and Work,* p. 69. Jones says that the Rank-Freud phase followed a Rank-Jones controversy. Jones and Rank had to work together in the management of the Committee's publications. Jones interprets Rank's growing dislike for him as "brother hostility."
18. See Ruth Munroe, *Schools of Psychoanalytic Thought* (New York: Dryden, 1955), pp. 575–600.
19. Ira Progoff, *The Death and Rebirth of Psychoanalysis* (New York: Julian, 1956), pp. 168–253. Freud started something but then killed it by his own reductionism, says Progoff. In Jung and Rank, notably, this something is reborn. Cf. Progoff, *Depth Psychology and Modern Man* (New York: Julian, 1959) especially at p. 62.

By this Rank seems to argue for recognition and affirmation not only of one's human nature with all its mystery and potential but also of the shared humanity, that of the community—or potential community—of mankind.[20] Alfred Adler, on a perhaps less "profound" level of insight, argues for what he calls "community feeling."[21]

It is easy to see, especially if one reads the lectures of A. A. Brill, the "first" American champion of Freudian psychology and controversial translator of his "basic writings" for American readers,[22] why Brill would report "in lurid terms" the strange doctrines which Rank was teaching in New York and "the confusion" he was creating among the congregations. The orthodox saw a heresy which struck at the roots of analytic therapy. Was it no longer necessary to analyze dreams, to go into sexual matters? Rank's view seemed to be a birth-trauma reductionism.[23]

Like Ferenczi, Rank emphasized love as the therapeutic agent in both psychotherapy and social melioration. He even used the theologian's term *agape*.[24] He referred to works by Martin Buber and Anders Nygren.[25] Of course, to read widely and to cite non-psychoanalytic writers were entirely within the tradition. However, in Rank, as in Horney,[26] for instance, such writers do more than simply serve to illustrate the analyst's point.

20. *Rank, Psychology and the Soul,* trans. William D. Turner (Philadelphia: University of Pennsylvania Press, 1950), pp. 91–93; *Beyond Psychology* (published privately by friends and students of author, Camden, N.J., 1941), pp. 17–61; 271–91. Progoff, *Death and Rebirth,* p. 229.
21. *Infra,* Chapter six will include more discussion of Adler.
22. *Lectures on Psychoanalytic Psychiatry* (New York: Alfred A. Knopf, 1946) and *Freud's Contribution to Psychiatry* (New York: W. W. Norton & Co., Inc., 1944). On Brill as translator, see Jones', *Life and Work,* Vol. 2, pp. 45–46.
23. *Ibid.,* Vol. 3, p. 71. Neither Brill nor Jones supplied the term *congregations,* however.
24. For instance, see *Beyond Psychology,* p. 175.
25. *Ibid.,* p. 290, for example (Buber); p. 175 (Nygren). Among other Christian scholars quoted is T. W. Manson, late Professor of New Testament studies at the University of Manchester.
26. E.g., Kierkegaard figures in Horney's *Our Inner Conflicts* (New York: W. W. Norton & Co., Inc., 1946) (at p. 183, for instance); also she was influenced somewhat by John Macmurray (his *Reason and Emotion* [London: Faber, 1935]).

Like Adler, Rank views the individual in a way which we often describe today as "holistic."[27] He treats the psyche as a unit, even though he seeks to avoid oversimplification by stressing the inner world of the irrational. Like Jung, he assumes that there is a mysterious depth of "the self" within every person, even though circumstances may prevent a true development of the potential for individual selfhood.[28] Rank is a voluntarist. The ego is will![29]

The theories of Rank are of interest to us in this stage of our inquiry not primarily because of his relationship with Freud nor because of his holistic presuppositions, although these facts are relevant. But he is introduced at length because of his distinctive emphasis on guilt, on what he termed "ethical guilt."[30]

Rank believes that the goal for the human being is to become individuated. The trauma is separation at birth. Also, at weaning and at other stages of development. After the *Geburtstrauma*, the basic injury, the matrix of anxiety itself, the individual is shaped by a succession of separation crises, none of which, of course, can really compare with that first one. There seems to be in the very nature of the separated being a capacity and potential for relative independence and self-reliance. After all, look how far he has come, even to be born into this world. From his very formation as an embryo, he has been destined not only to separation but to

27. The term derives from Jan Christian Smuts' *Holism and Evolution* (New York: Macmillan, 1926).
28. *Beyond Psychology*, p. 289. There are many passages that make the point.
29. Rank's holism, despite some vagueness about it, as illustrated by his use of the term *"spiritual"* is seen in his concept of will. He defines it as "an autonomous organizing force in the individual which does not represent any particular biological impulse or social drive but constitutes the creative expression of the total personality and distinguishes one individual from another." *Ibid.*, p. 50.
30. Otto Rank, "Truth and Reality," (in *Will Therapy and Truth and Reality*, trans. Jessie Taft (New York: Alfred A. Knopf, 1945), pp. 209–305. "Separation and Guilt," *Ibid.*, pp. 71–85.
Rank's concept of ethical guilt is reminiscent of Søren Kierkegaard in *The Concept of Dread*, trans. Walter Lowrie (Princeton: Princeton University Press, 1957), especially when "SK" speaks of "the dread in which the individual posits sin by the qualitative leap; and the dread which entered in along with sin, and which for this reason comes also into the world quantitatively every time an individual posits sin." (p. 49). One becomes and is what he does. There is dread in the doing. Otto Rank focused again on this aspect of behavior.

individuation. These are as much a part of the logic—and psychology—of human existence as are union and dependence.

The tragedy is that narrow is the way and few there be who find it. Many persons will go so far, but only to come pathetically short of the possibility which is implied in their very nature. They who miss the way range from "average man" (a favorite term of Rank) to the neurotic, psychotic, and psychopathic.

The elect, as it were, are those who are creative in their response to the challenge of individuation in the midst of separation anxiety. Rank calls these the "artist" types.[31] The "neurotic" and the "artist" are alike in one respect: both recognize the awful fact of separation—from the womb and from the herd. The average man somehow fails ever to assimilate this fact. He rejects the truth in the fact of separation and the implicit possibility of individuation. He refuses to tolerate ethical guilt. Thus Rank explains both mob psychology and slavish conformity. The average man escapes the terrifying awareness of his separateness by incorporating unreflectively the views of his society, regardless of what they happen to be. He cannot bear the thought of being in any sense cut off from the fictional unity which he supposes in society. Here we are reminded of recent tracts of the times, beginning, say, with David Riesman's study of the individual and the crowd.[32]

Rank's theory developed in much greater depth perhaps than did his therapeutic technique, which he called "will therapy." His emphasis on the will, on the conscious mind, and on a much shorter length of time for analysis than that which the old-line Freudians tend to require, reminds us of Alfred Adler's, which like Rank's, was appreciated by many social workers and counselling psychologists who cannot think in terms of long courses of treatment.[33]

---

31. Rank's intellectual history is marked by a preoccupation with the "artist." His first book was *Der Kunstler* (1907). Later, this designation was given to what he considered healthy humanity because it can convey "a sense of creative integration as the highest goal of man" (Munroe, *Schools of Psychoanalytic Thought,* p. 586).
32. David Riesman et al., *The Lonely Crowd* (New Haven: Yale University Press, 1950).
33. See Munroe, *Schools of Psychoanalytic Thought,* pp. 588–94.

Psychogenetically the will emerges as counter-will. Here there seems to be a correlation with the infancy crisis (and crises) that we see expounded in Suttie and Erikson. Counter-will emerges with the small child's discovery of his power to say "No" and to frustrate the desires of his environment, his society, which, to Rank, is the will against which he develops his own.

As the infant grows, he gradually abandons his efforts to re-create through fantasy his recent intra-uterine state. He gradually comes to experience himself as a totality. This self as the I of self-recognition is what Rank seems to mean by the will. As it emerges it is largely negative, behaving *vis-à-vis* the will which it experiences as acting upon it from the outside world.

Not only can the child say "No" to others, he can refuse his own impulses. Hence, we may understand the frequent cutting-off-the-nose-to-spite-the-face behavior of small children (and others not so small). What is happening is the fascinating development of a new individuality. Thrown more and more on his own by the fact of increasing relative separation, the small child begins to rise to the occasion, to assume the responsibility for what he does. He is becoming, however gradually, a person in his own right in the world of personalities which he finds around him. Rankian therapy values the counter-will for individuation above the goals of personal happiness and social adjustment, which are often based on the illusion held by the average-man type. Therapy has a higher calling than to turn out average men. Service to the highest value is the mission of Rank's will therapy, which he likens to a kind of psychic obstetrics: bringing—with a minimum of birth trauma —into the world of reality creative individuals ready to take the risks of anxiety and ethical guilt.

What is the role of guilt feeling in the process of individuation? Rank says that any assertion of counter-will necessarily arouses feelings of anxiety, specifically the form of anxiety which is commonly described as guilt. Guilt feeling is essentially fear of separation. Hence, we see, says Rank, guilt feeling is at once inevitable and healthy if the person is to fulfill his destiny and become individuated.

Like Sullivan, Rank takes pains to distinguish what he means by proper guilt feeling from other phenomena that bear the label "guilt." The necessary guilt which is incurred by allowing the counter-will to develop is to be distinguished always from that feeling which one has when he has committed an act which is considered as wrong according to some code, whether society's or his own. This latter guilt, which characteristically is in the service of blind conformity, is what Rank calls "moralistic guilt." It also is inevitable. The very fact that the individual finds himself in society means that the collective will presents itself to him in the form of code, to be sure, but also, in the internalized code, his conscience. We see here that Rank has not forgotten his Freud.

But ethical guilt is a much deeper problem. It accompanies any expression of one's own will as it distinguishes itself from that of the environment or of any important segment thereof. But a person feels ethical guilt also when he complies with the outside will. He is guilty of offending his own will—the counter-will to that of the outside.

Guilt feeling is unavoidable if one is either self-assertive or self-denying. It represents the tension between separation and union. Union was and is good. But the separateness is also good. It has its blessings and opportunities. To offend either principle is to be the victim of the appropriate anxiety: separation from others or separation from one's own developing individuality. That individuality soon comes to represent quite an emotional investment. It has come to stand for both security and meaning in one's own existence.

The injunction of a responsible ethics, as well as that of Rankian therapy, may indeed be: Take courage and live with ethical guilt. We recall Martin Luther's dictum: "Therefore sin bravely." Significantly, to Rank, the greater sin is to refuse to risk the anxiety of separation, the inevitable guilt one feels if he tries to become what he by nature is destined to be, an individual. Rank's avowedly soteriological concern is to save both the neurotic and the average man from the fate which George Bernard Shaw has described as simply being lived by one's life. "Salvation" is "unto life": life is lived by an *individual* who is in responsible relationship with others.

Like Horney, Rank is reminiscent of the early theologian Paul —who himself also went through a separation ordeal while already in the midst of a career, whose "will therapy" is articulated in an essay written in the latter part of the first century C. E.: "Be not conformed to this world." But then the apostle of that era went on to introduce another will into the injunction. Even without being de-theologized, Paul's theme can be taken as at least analogous to the evangel of the newly liberated Otto Rank.

5

Freedom and Responsibility:

Guilt Feelings and

Human Development

Even Freudians, like Edmund Bergler, find themselves positing two consciences: the oppressive superego and the "conscience."[1] Ernest Jones insists that good Freudian theory never dropped the concept of ego ideal, distinguished from the superego, which Freud introduced in the early 1920's. Bergler regards the superego as the repressed conscience, the unconscious devil in everyone. The healthy conscience is formed by pre-Oedipal identifications with good objects.

Conflict rages in everyone. The question is not whether conscience, but what kind. The child is bound to develop ideas of good and evil. The answer does not lie in attempts to avoid or deny a sense of badness in the child. As Erik Erikson says, "The denial of the unavoidable can only deepen a sense of secret, unmanageable evil."[2] He argues that the answer is in the ego's capacity to create order. If this is encouraged, then the conscience of tomorrow can be both disciplined and tolerant and the world can be ordered to suit the life-affirming "psychological man."[3]

The crises of human development, epitomized in the identity crisis, involve not only love, fear, and their combining in guilt, but also compulsive hostility which often strikes out offensively, as in familiar episodes of juvenile violence, and less tragic youthful aggression against both ideological and human targets. Erikson explains some of Luther's verbal excesses by this general observa-

1. Edmund Bergler, *The Superego: Unconscious Conscience* (New York: Grune & Stratton, 1952).
2. *Young Man Luther*, p. 263.
3. A phrase which Philip Rieff likes to use; e.g., in his *Freud: The Mind of the Moralist* (New York: Viking Press, 1959), pp. 261–392.

tion. He calls it the necessity to repudiate. It is part of the process of individuation.

The need to repudiate is the reverse side of the need to devote oneself to something. The small child, like the adolescent, is looking for a way of devotion. His repudiating behavior is often but a part of this process of testing the possibilities for identification. In trying to resolve his identity crisis, which often continues through the years of adolescence, the individual devotes himself, perhaps by fits and starts, to a variety of causes. He may change quickly from one loyalty to another, repudiating today what he would have given his life for yesterday. The need to repudiate may persist into the twenties and even beyond. It manifests itself even when there may be no explicit ideological commitment or interest. This may explain the sometimes puzzling phenemenon of young people offering devotion to individual leaders, teams, singers, to activities and techniques that call for sacrifice and concentration, which may seem to the older, or objective, observer to be hardly worth such effort. At the same time, the youth who is still struggling with his identity problem is likely to show "a sharp and intolerant readiness to discard and disavow people" including, at times, himself. "This repudiation is often snobbish, fitful, perverted, or simply thoughtless."[4]

Erikson illustrates the point with prominent examples like Augustine and Freud, who choose moratoria of the resolution of the crisis, who "do not necessarily *know* that they are marking time before they come to their crossroad, which they often do in the late twenties, belated just because they gave their all to the temporary subject of devotion." We recall that Freud was a laboratory physiologist for some years, more or less deliberately putting off the completion of his medical training. "The crisis in such a young man's life may be reached exactly when he half-realizes that he is fatally overcommitted to what he is not."[5]

In his attempt to achieve identity, the individual often settles for a time of diffusion of role, a diffusion of identity. During this

4. *Young Man Luther,* pp. 42–43.
5. *Ibid.*

period he may feel that he is committed to a cause which will catch his whole being up into its meaning and fulfillment. Luther's calm period, according to Erikson, was right after he went to the monastery. We are reminded of the guilt feeling which Rank says is inevitable in the process of individuation, as we read Erikson's description of Luther during this era of diffused identity:

> Most of all, this kind of person must shy away from intimacy. And physical closeness, with either sex, arouses at the same time both an impulse to merge with the other person and a fear of losing autonomy and individuation.[6]

Ideological leaders, who are likely to be among those whose identity crisis is prolonged, seem to be "subject to excessive fears which they can master only by reshaping the thoughts of their contemporaries; while those contemporaries are always glad to have their thoughts shaped by those who desperately care to do so." Perhaps our readiest example is the Third Reich with its Adolf Hitler. Erikson does not miss this one, even in his study of Luther, who was spiritual leader for the same ethnic community four centuries earlier.[7] He offers impressive documentation for his thesis that Hitler was suffering from an unresolved identity crisis, in which the negative aspect of the devotion-repudiation dynamism was dominant, and tragically, due to the times and circumstances it was allowed to harness itself to a powerful potential, the German nation.

Hitler's childhood reveries were dominated by the impulse to tear down and rebuild. From fifteen to nineteen he was pre-occupied specifically with the idea of tearing down certain buildings in his hometown of Linz and rebuilding them according to elaborate plans which he himself drew up. He was especially interested in destroying and rebuilding the opera house there. In fact, it has been discovered, says Erikson, that he had returned to

---

6. *Ibid.*, p. 101.
7. *Ibid.*, pp. 105–9. An earlier study, "Hitler's Imagery and German Youth," *Psychiatry*, V, (1942), pp. 475–93 was reprinted in Clyde Kluckhorn and Henry A. Murray, eds., *Personality: Its Nature, Society, and Culture* (New York: Alfred A. Knopf, 1948). See also "The Legend of Hitler's Childhood," in *Childhood and Society*, Chap. 9, pp. 284–315.

this specific preoccupation shortly before his death.[8] He was emotionally and psychologically fifteen, drawing plans for a new opera house after he had destroyed it—that is, satisfied the urge to repudiate it. The fact is all the more painful when we realize that Hitler turned to political matters only after he had been refused admission to a school of architecture.[9]

Was the Hitler whom Erikson presents struggling with ethical guilt while he was trying to find his identity? In other words, are the Rankian and Eriksonian models compatible? Do Erikson's crises, identity, intimacy, generativity, and integrity resemble Rank's struggle for individuation—being an individual in responsible relationship? Is the leader who fails to resolve his identity problem an artist or a neurotic? Are the many who do resolve their identity problem in relative composure anything like the Rankian "average man"? Perhaps we are better off not to mix the frames of reference but simply to recognize both complementary and contradictory possibilities for the two when they are seen together.

According to Erikson, the parental environment provides the first image for identification striving. Does devotion to the image entail guilt because of the offended ego, or that particular segment of the ego which feels negated by any compliance with the parent image? Repudiation results from the *coup* effected by this guilt. The counter-will gains only partial control over the person's situation. The parental will is internalized. This is analogous to the ego and superego dichotomy which Rank had followed in his Freudian days. In an analogy, the ego takes on two aspects, that of the elder brother who identifies with the parental will, and the prodigal who demands his portion of the inheritance.[10] The elder brother within takes offense at the independence-seeking prodigal ego. The parable of the father and his two sons can also be used to suggest the kind of integration that is the desideratum; reconciliation between the inner forces of dependence and independence; that is, accord-

---

8. Cf. Albert Speer, *Inside the Third Reich,* trans. Richard and Clara Winston (New York: Macmillan & Co., 1970), p. 298 and *passim.*
9. *Young Man Luther,* pp. 105–9; Cf. *Childhood and Society,* pp. 284–315.
10. Luke 15:11–32.

ing to Erikson, when one has successfully internalized the father (parents)-son (child) relationship.[11]

Erikson's view of "integration" suggests resolution or synthesis as the prospect for the healthy individual. Rank, however, reminds us of Kierkegaard. Perhaps for the moment we may liken Erikson to Hegel. The Rankian man is in a never ending struggle for individuation-in-relationship, which is an essential dichotomy. If the human being is to be a human being he must live in a state of tension. Rank calls this ethical guilt; it is the Janus-faced gateway to every action—will versus counter-will writ into the very psyche of the social being. Erikson posits a negative conscience, a dark side we might say, versus a positive, or bright side. Rank posits a dual conscience: against separation, on the one hand, and against union, on the other and at the same time. We can put this positively, perhaps, and say that there is a conscience that favors individuation and there is a conscience that favors relationship.

Generally, depth psychologists seem to agree that for man-in-society some guilt feeling is to be expected, and that regardless of whether it is to be regarded as good, bad, or neither, it should be utilized therapeutically in two directions: (1) toward healthy integration or individuation of the self; and (2) toward healthy relationship with the social environment, although therapists differ in how they regard such a goal.

Guilt feeling is a form of fear, or what is called anxiety. It presupposes a prior relationship, hence, in some measure, love. Guilt feeling asserts for the subject that he is beholden to someone or to society—and "to God." In Rank's theory, and, also in Horney's, the most important "someone" is the person himself. He can feel guilty toward himself.

In asking: What is the nature of guilt? we have sifted various answers. We have now to probe further into the emotions of guilt and shame, distinguishing them from each other as we can. Then we must search out in more detail the implications of anxiety,

11. *Young Man Luther, passim,* and pp. 213–16.: Cf. Rank, in "Forms of Kinship and the Individual's Role," in *The Myth of the Birth of the Hero and Other Writings* (New York: Alfred A. Knopf, 1959), pp. 296–315.

which antedates both shame and guilt in the development of human emotion. Such inquiry will bring us to the psychology of despair, a condition in which destructive emotions seem to have done their lethal work almost to the finish against the self.

6

The Complications of Shame Feelings

As we have seen, guilt feeling may be described as a fusion of fear, love, and hatred-turned-inward. It is a compulsion to make restitution, to effect a restoration, to be justified. The theories we have discussed in the preceding chapter have recognized the importance of this feeling of guilt both in emotional illness and in the normal development of personality.

Alfred Adler, a Vienna physician, was the first disciple—he himself would prefer the designation "colleague"—to leave Freud. Adler in his own right came to have a considerable influence on psychotherapy, educational psychology, and social work, especially in the United States and Great Britain, where he died, in 1937 while in Aberdeen to give a series of lectures.

We shall look at his psychology now, because of the curious omission of an emphasis on "guilt" in the structure of his thought. He approaches the etiology of neurosis with a sense of biology but also of sociology. Though he calls his psychology "individual" his aim in therapy is to bring the patient into social equilibrium. Although he says little about guilt feelings as such, he does teach a doctrine of responsibility.

His writings consist largely of addresses and monographs, all illustrating the same relatively clear-cut hypothesis. We can see the point at once when we approach Adler's work, more so perhaps than in any of the other theorists we are considering. He can say, in one brief preface:

Individual psychology covers the whole range of psychology in one survey, and as a result it is able to mirror the indivisible unity of the personality . . . . we modestly lay claim to the formulation of fundamental principles which have hereto never found expression in psychological literature . . . all forms of neurosis and developmental failure are expressions of inferiority and disappointment. . . . We individual psychologists are in a position, if a proper procedure is observed, to get a clear conception of the fundamental psychic error of the patient at the first consultation. And the way to cure is thus opened.[1]

In searching out the basic causes of neurosis, Adler presupposing the essential unity of the human "psyche," perceives the infant organism as it must compare itself with its towering environment. The feelings of discomfort, the "fear of degradation," of "lack of knowledge and orientation," the feeling of want, the frustrations related to using the sense organs and mechanisms of speech, lack of cleanliness, relative invalidism and the consequent fear of death are added up to make what he calls the feeling of being beneath, the feeling of uncertainty. These negative emotions are what compose the "infantile feelings of inferiority."[2]

The infant-child-adult is striving in a social milieu. This very fact means that he is working to overcome, to compensate for, that inner awareness of being beneath others. "I am vulnerable to accident, illness, open abasement." Hence, as he is hurled forward in a developing life, he should become, through the very process of growth and imposed adjustments, actually less inferior, at least to the infantile state. Yet he maintains an unrelenting inner sense of inferiority! It is a feeling of dependence which he somehow rejects as degrading.

Naturally, normally, inevitably, the infant will feel weak and helpless. But normal, healthy growth should mean non-neurotic adjustment. Although Adler, as a physician, was concerned with the "healing" of neuroses and prevention, he produced in his philosophical-psychological fragments an anthropology which presupposed the universality of the feeling of inferiority.

Adler's early research into the problem of organic inferiority was recognized by Freud as an important contribution to the new science of depth psychology.[3] The master felt, however, that his

1. *The Practice and Theory of Individual Psychology,* trans. Paul Radin (London: Kegan Paul, Trench, & Trubner, 1924), pp. v–vi.

2. *The Neurotic Constitution,* trans. Bernard Glueck and John Lind (New York: Moffat Yard, 1917), p. 73.

3. However, Freud's faint praise of Adler is found in the critical demolition he presents in "On the History of the Psycho-Analytic Movement," in *Complete Psychology Works,* trans. Joan Riviere, Vol. 14 (London: Hogarth, 1930), p. 51.

erstwhile collaborator had substituted the appendix for the body of truth when he began to spin his inclusive theory from the research. Adler, in turn, felt that Freud had failed to see the "lowest common denominator" of the causes of neurosis as the sense of inferiority.[4] He came to feel that for the therapist's purposes the unconscious could be discerned clearly enough through the conscious behavior and in the pattern or style of life of the patient.

This feeling of inferiority is linked with the fact that the individual is biologically bisexual in a culture that tends to regard masculinity as normative! Here we can see in Adler the same general orientation we see in Sigmund Freud. Both are temperamentally patriarchal in their approach to sex differences. At least, it would seem so, during the days of their collaboration and immediately following. Adler links inferiority with femininity, while Freud links fears and envy over the lack of a penis in the girl and the threat of castration felt by the boy.

Today as we read Adler, and to some extent even as we read Freud, we question how really necessary is this emphasis on masculinity for the overall logic of either system. As we have seen, Ian Suttie, Karen Horney, and we could add, C. G. Jung and Otto Rank and many others, emphasize the positive aspects of femininity; it is to be envied rather than abhorred.

The feeling of inferiority demands a compensation before what Adler calls "ego-consciousness." An imagined goal is established, which he calls a "fiction." Adler was influenced by Hans Vaihinger's *Philosophy of 'As If'*;[5] it provided him with a philosophical foundation for his doctrine. Vaihinger called his position "idealistic positivism." His approach seems compatible with American pragmatism. To Adler, the individual lives by a philosophy of "as if." It is at once a fiction and a goal which direct him, a compensatory fiction and goal. Life and growth mean that there is a special force at work bent on making compensation for the feeling of inferiority. Adler correlated this force with that which

---

4. See, for instance, Heinz L. and Rowena R., Ansbacher, *The Individual Psychology of Alfred Adler* (New York: Basic Books, 1956), pp. 16–22.
5. Berlin, 1911.

Nietzsche recognized as the "will to power."[6] The preoccupation of every mortal is the negative conviction about his own worth and the solving of this problem of inferiority. Regardless of how it may manifest itself, this is the problem.

Instead of the Freudian stages, there are simply three, which are essentially the same crisis, the triple encounter of the individual with his social environment. They are: (1) the crisis of establishing oneself in a meaningful relationship with society, (2) the crisis of establishing oneself in a love relationship, and (3) the crisis of establishing oneself in an occupation which assures one of significance.

How well a person resolves each of these crises depends on how he is introduced to society, love, and tools while he is a small child—already within a family style–of–life. Neurotic, psychotic, and criminal behavior indicate failure to mount one or more of these related hurdles. It is common for one to try, at least in his imagination, to alter the loved partner, even to substitute fantasy or compulsion entirely for reality in the sphere of love. It is common for one to place highly unrealistic constructions upon his own occupation in life.[7] However, earlier than either of these two fictional attempts at resolving a crisis of encounter, the individual has already found his meaningful relationship with society as he himself imagines and delimits it in his own mind.

Adler became a kind of preacher, a social ideologist. He worked toward the goal of social "inter-cooperation," mutually edifying love relationships, and progress-making occupation for the patient, and for mankind. By temperament, he liked to be optimistic, positive, constructive. Nevertheless, he realized that society measured by his ideals was sick.

The will to power, the drive for compensation, can be largely transformed by therapy into the will to cooperate. Human beings should learn to strive for the happiness of others. "It is more

6. Adler, *The Neurotic Constitution*, p. 24.
7. See Adler's discussions in such popular treatments as *The Science of Living* (London: George Allen & Unwin, 1930), pp. 199–262; and *What Life Should Mean to You*, ed. Alan Porter (London: George Allen & Unwin, 1932), pp. 252–86.

blessed to give than to receive," Adler liked to quote from the New Testament.[8] Through education and re-educative therapy cooperation can transplant superiority striving.

As we have seen, the fiction which the infant ego sets up, is a reversal of inferiority. The goal is seen in the vision of an ideal self—the "self ideal," which stands for a continual feeling of being above.[9] These feelings of being above are composed of such wished-for attainments as joy, victory, knowledge, wealth, art, cleanliness, life envisioned as immortality, and esteem.[10]

The ego refuses to take its situation lying down, so to speak. While the infant maintains a measure of "the eternal, real and physiologically rooted 'community-feeling'" from which "are developed tenderness, love of neighbor, friendship and love," he cannot bear the feeling of inferiority which seems to be his lot.[11] This painful and negative feeling takes different forms with different individuals, according to the nature of the organic inferiority, the neurotic compensations which are sought by other members of the family—often at the infant's expense—and the general impact of the initial encounter with the environment. The sense of inferiority thus objectified in the individual's own infantile idiom declares its opposite simply by removing the negatives. "Whatever I am not I shall be" expresses at once the goal and the lust for power. Hence, the style-of-life manifests the as-if attitude which demands the fruits of superiority even though it has never been achieved.

This fictional goal is a positive image created out of a negative reality. The infant is in fact inferior to the adult. What is more,

8. Acts 20:35. See *Understanding Human Nature,* trans. Walter Beran Wolfe (London: George Allen & Unwin, 1927), p. 211; also pp. 33–43; and *passim.*

9. Of course Adler came to make a more favorable impression on others than he had on Freud in using such phrasing. "Adler . . . positively considers that the strongest motive force in the sexual act is the man's intention of showing himself master of the woman—of being 'on top.' I do not know if he has expressed these monstrous notions in his writings." (Freud, "On the History of the Psycho-Analytic Movement," p. 53.)

10. Cf. Adler's diagram, presented in *The Neurotic Constitution,* p. 73.

11. *Individual Psychology,* p. 9.

everyone, the adult included, is more or less inferior to his fellows in some regard. There is no denying this. Nor can it be denied that everyone rebels inwardly against his own inferiority. It may not be an oversimplification to suggest that this inner rebellion finds unmistakable expression in a relentless drive for mastery, a lust for power which must be understood in the context of the individual's own private world of inner conflict. But, according to Adler, such power-crazed rebellion, however it may be disguised in neurosis, psychosis, criminality, or inoffensive complacent dream-world satisfaction, is in fact trying to establish the ego in the haven of the "self ideal," to uproot inferiority-feeling and to plant a certainty of superiority. This superiority is in form, though not in essence, over others. It is a vision of a triumphant opposite to the inferiority which terrorized the infant. But its sweep fells others along with the despised image of one's own inferior self. Hence it is anti-social, detrimental to the common goal, at least in motivation. Adler sees it as the source of social evil.[12] His optimism is that although such a motivation is practically universal, its evil effects do not have to dominate the individual. The community feeling should be evoked to counteract them successfully.

He tells us that we must face the fact that "this fiction of a goal of superiority so ridiculous from the view-point of reality, has become the principal conditioning factor of our life as hitherto known."[13] According to Adler, it is the setting up of this fiction which introduces hostility and aggressiveness into one's behavior.

Yet, there is a positive side to the dynamics of superiority-striving. It "teaches us to differentiate, gives us poise and forces our spirit to look ahead and to perfect ourselves." It is interesting to compare this statement with one by a Freudian, Margaret Harries, in "Sublimation in a Group of Four-Year-Old Boys."

12. *Ibid.*, p. 8. Cf. *What Life Should Mean to You*, p. 69, where Adler makes a characteristic statement stressing the positive aspects of superiority striving and cooperation.
13. *Individual Psychology, loc. cit.*, where the statement appears in italics.

"The impulses originally causing the children to indulge in unacceptable behavior are the same ones which later provide the driving force of their socially acceptable and enjoyable activities, namely, the aggressive drives and the pregenital component instincts."[14]

To Adler, the individual becomes caught up in a plan of life, or "life style," which spells out the nature of the inferiority and of the imagined goal. Armed with such knowledge, the therapist attempts to re-educate the patient, carrying him back—as in other kinds of psychoanalysis—to the origin of the neurosis, where he can see with adult eyes the infantilism of the inferiorities felt and feared at the dawn of ego consciousness. The patient, all the while feeling the encouraging support of his therapist-friend, should then be able to recognize his self-ideal as a simple goal of superiority, utterly impossible of achievement.[15]

This encounter of therapist and patient (client) may be interpreted as the community's meeting with the individual to bring about the reconciliation needed. The original alienation of the self is from his social environment. Although the inferiority feeling has its biological and organic basis, it is social in its effect, and the "self ideal" is social in its content. Adler is really talking about the problem of identity—the question: Who am I in this world of other bodies?—and relating it to pre-Oedipal (we would have to say, if forced to translate to a Freudian frame of reference) conflict within the self's consciousness. The situation implies a "knowledge of good and evil" which is painful to the ego. Indeed it is not to be tolerated. Therefore, in order to protect the self (the self's "idea" or "image" of itself) from the suffering that goes with feeling looked down upon, inferior, expendable, ashamed all

---

14. The article is in Ruth S. Eissler et al., *The Psycho-analytic Study of the Child,* Vol. 7 (London and New York: International Universities Press, 1952), pp. 230–40.

15. Heinz L. and Rowena R. Ansbacher in their systematic presentation of Adler's thought and writings, say that he introduced the term "guiding self ideal" in 1912, in *The Neurotic Constitution,* where, "to all appearances, he used it interchangeably with 'the fictional goal.'" (*Individual Psychology,* p. 95.) Freud formulated his "ideal ego" in "On Narcissism," (1914).

the time "of being me," the volitional dynamism known as the individual adopts an as-if portrait which he superimposes on his mirror. This, Adler calls the haven of the self ideal. With it, the ego's *modus vivendi* is to try to confirm the portrait definition, not the one which it fears would lie behind it in the mirror. Hence, it is a risky business, tearing that portrait off and exposing the mirror. Can one bear such knowledge?

The ego holds on to the portrait with considerable force. That energy is like that—perhaps identifiable with it—which the infant– child-adult has directed as hostile aggressiveness against the social environment to which he has felt inferior. The goal of superiority striving has been to turn the tables, reverse the positions, according to Adler. It is the fiction that the last shall be first and that the first shall be last, that the inferior, insecure infant becomes the superior, secure adult who can look down his nose at that environment which he has felt looking down on him. To Adler, the beings in the Garden are not content to sew for themselves fig leaves and to try to hide from the most high. They go on attempting to "be like the most high." It is doubtful whether the reconciliation can be so simple as the providing of garments of skins and a blunt confirmation of their eviction from Eden or telling them that they were never there in the first place!

Yet, Adler holds that the reconciliation does involve the over- coming of fiction with fact. But the fact must be a new—yes, a redemptive—fact. It must be the practical undoing of the terror and tyranny of the inferiority feeling. He thinks this is possible by what he calls patient "re-education" of the individual by society's surrogate, the therapist. Such re-education is possible because of the individual's innate community feeling.

We are reminded of the later and Freudian constructions of Melanie Klein. She teaches that neurosis can be prevented by early environmental support to the "love instincts" in their struggle with the "death instincts." She preaches a gospel of psychoanalysis, envisioning what it can do for character and for the world. Its work of lessening infantile anxiety "not only lessens and modifies the child's aggressive impulses but leads to a more valuable employment and gratification of them from a social point of view." With such educative, supportive, attention, "the child shows an ever-growing, deeply rooted desire to be loved and to love, and to be at peace with the world about it."[16]

Of course, Adler tries to avoid Freudian instinctual dualism. Nevertheless, it is not without warrant that Adlerians think that they perceive in Freud's introduction of such a doctrine a belated —if distorted—recognition of the point which Adler was making when he left Freud's circle. Adler preferred to define the polarity in terms of goals: superiority of the self versus community. Nevertheless, he recognized the inwardness of the conflict: it is between two feelings: inferiority feeling and community feeling. Yet, he insisted that the energy for both feelings was the same. The question is one of direction not of hopelessly alienated drives.

To Adler the social philosopher-tractarian, the good is whatever makes for both individual and social well-being. He tended to presuppose that the two are essentially compatible. The inferiority feeling complains that an offense of privation has been committed against the self at the very dawn of life. This is privation by comparison. The infant compares himself with others. He gets off on the wrong track. Why not bring him around to a realistic view of himself and his society?

When we collate Adler with Rank we have to ask: Is Adler's power-seeking neurotic, when converted into a cooperative, community-oriented individual not likely to be more Rank's average man—little better off than his neurotic—instead of the truly realistic, and optimally healthy "artist?"

We have already contrasted Suttie with Adler on the questions of motivation and goal in the crises of human development. Suttie teaches that the reconciliation with society means the overcoming by it of the individual's hatred produced in the traumatic ordeal of psychic weaning. The state from which the infant has fallen is the paradigm for love as giving and receiving in the community, namely, the symbiotic relationship of mother and infant. The

16. Melanie Klein, "The Early Development of Conscience in the Child," reprinted in *Contributions to Psycho-Analysis,* 1921–1941 (London: Hogarth, 1948), pp. 267–77 and in *Psychoanalysis Today,* ed. Sandor Lorand (New York: International Universities Press, 1944), pp. 67–75.

individual's alienation can be overcome in therapy because of the agency of active, reassuring, supportive "love." Horney agrees that the form of such love is therapeutic expression of acceptance instead of rejection of the individual's "real self" and re-education.

Perhaps there is but one string on Adler's fiddle. But on it he can play this kind of tune: the important thing is that the individual feel good about himself. If he does then he can feel good about society. If the feeling good requires that he feel superior, then he is still hiding himself from the real world and his own real self.

Obviously, Adler ascribes a quality of reality to both the community and the self which presupposes something like the religious notions of "kingdom of God," and "new humanity." Indeed, it is easy to translate Adler into any of several varieties of liberal theology. For instance, the "neurotic life style" is like the "state of sin," or the "Adamic nature." He propounds a doctrine of conversion to community-seeking, and away from destructiveness (walking in the darkness of one's fiction about his own identity). By receiving insight, the Adlerian man leaves his fictional way of life. He learns to accept both his weaknesses and his strengths— this is like Luther's discovery of the Pauline doctrine of "justification by faith alone." Implicit in Adler's teaching is the doctrine of grace. The new man, the re-educated self, henceforth lives for the greater cause, the good of the idealized community; this is like Luther's conception of Christian liberty.

Yet, as we noted at the beginning of this chapter, this gospeler calls us not to a confession of our guilt or even of the fact that we feel guilty. But our illness is due to our feeling of shame. We are called to renounce our fictional glory by reassessing the reason for it. Perhaps it is time now to look a bit further at this condition of "soul" which logically, if not psychologically, antecedes guilt feeling. Adler, seconded by Horney and others, forces upon us a fresh recognition of the importance of what we so easily might take for granted. In waking to life the nascent ego witnesses a power of the environment which seems to increase while his own power seems relatively to decrease. His omnipotence fantasies appear to him increasingly to be mere fantasies. To grow in realism means to be pared down in size and glory. There is a sense of loss—even at the dawn of what we call consciousness. This is evidenced clinically in the frequent allusion by patients to child-hood memories that feature something being taken away: the pattern of associations may include bicycles, candy canes, a favor-ite doll, a ball that could never be found, a playmate, or a favorite adult presence. A part of the price of maintaining and further developing a sense of I-ness, or individuation, is to mourn for the loss of something. "There hath passed away a glory from the earth."[17] In saying this we need not kid ourselves, we need not hold on to our little homemade fictions about glory regained. Adler seems to reveal that he himself has taken a leap of faith: there is in our lives a grace that is sufficient for us, whose strength can be brought to perfection even in our weakness.

17. William Wordsworth, "Intimations of Immortality from Recollections of Early Childhood."

7

The Significance of Shame Feelings

The teaching of various schools of depth psychology about separation, as the formative cause of emotional conflict, posits an early sense of deprivation. Perhaps hopefulness itself and preoccupation with "new heavens and new earth" can be at least partially explained by the memory of Eden, a state before the near-crippling awareness of privation.

If we follow Melanie Klein, Freud himself, C. G. Jung, with his belief in determinative archetypes, and Rank, in their contrasting ways, we place the primal sense of privation no later than the moment of birth. Freud with his persistent belief in a phylogenetic fall, seems to imply that the deprivation feeling is programmed into the embryo-psyche itself.

To Karen Horney, the "basic anxiety" is separation anxiety. It is not a sense of organ inferiority or body inferiority, primarily, but separation fear, in a social sense. Ian Suttie, quite independently, propounds a similar view. However, he tries to preserve the recognition of somatic—biological—factors which relate to this ordeal of separation and the fears which it engenders. Otto Rank, as we have seen, builds on the idea of separation.

According to Horney, the "basic anxiety" arises in the experience, or pattern of experiences, which the child interprets as rejection. He feels rejected by his parent or parent surrogate. To be sure, his feeling, and his growing habit of feeling that he is rejected may, to a large extent, be a subjective misconstruction of the remembered event which comes to symbolize rejection and separation. There may be room in such a theory for phylogenetic and somatic etiology, but Horney, like Sullivan, stresses the interpersonal aspects of the experience from cause to cure.

Horney's "idealized self image" ("ideal self") is like Adler's "fiction of superiority" and "self ideal." Her idea of trends, personality type, and personality structure suggest his concept of life style. Adler's influence is marked in Horney, Rank, and ego psychologists like Erikson who speak of "style of life."

To Freudians, the ego ideal as posited before the doctrine of an Oedipally-induced superego is a construct within the ego that depends not so much upon a dynamics of guilt as upon what we may call a dynamics of shame.

To Adler, the infant ego inevitably comes to the conclusion that the self is deprived to begin with, hopelessly behind in the game as he enters it. Somehow convince him that he is worth something, although he is inferior to his composite milieu, and you solve his problem and the problem that he may be for society. Do this for enough persons and the problems of society are solved. Overcome in the individual the one-talent-servant mentality and its variations. Then he can live both creatively and realistically. He will be using a new interpretation of his recognition of failure.

Horney sees rejection as the operative form of both separation and deprivation. Man is built to endure the thousand natural shocks that flesh is heir to. Can he endure the insult of parental rejection which is added to the injury? Rejection threatens his security, his sense of at-one-ness with his world. Because that world is overwhelming in its magnitude and power, his feeling that he is being cut off from it, or in danger of being cut off, is tantamount to being put out with the rubbish. Is he rubbish, a mere nothing, worthless?

Freudians see the effect on the adult personality in the failure of the ego to surmount any one of the crises of infancy and early childhood. The threat is always from forces seemingly bent on destroying the person either from within or from the outside world. Guilt characterizes the individual who has at least partially resolved the pre-Oedipal crises. Generally, the failure to emerge whole from infancy into childhood is due to previous failures to win through on trust over mistrust or on will power over the sense of shame (inferiority) and doubt. The ego has become realized at some earlier stage. In Melanie Klein's world of split objects, the failure of the infant to overcome evil objects with good ones in the inner pantheon results in despair, or pessimism, indeed, often, a driving, terrifying sense of futility.

It would seem, therefore, that the privilege of being able to feel what these psychologists call guilt is open only to those who have not been overcome by insecurity and shame. Reverting again to the helpful latticework which the ego-psychologist Erik Erikson provides, we may say that a protracted crisis of identity (Erikson's version of Freud's Oedipal crisis) reflects the fact that the obstacle shame has never been successfully removed from the path to meaningful identification and integration of the self. Internalized ego ideals dominate a weak ego. Some apparently selfless persons are leaners, who try, perhaps not quite consciously, to be a part of someone else's psyche, someone else's destiny, because their own is so impoverished.

Harry Stack Sullivan says that the "waking self" cannot accept as truly a part of the self dynamism the dissociated shameful or not-me elements which are left along the trail of development. As Patrick Mullahy faithfully expounds Sullivan's view:

> The self may be said to be made up of or at least circumscribed by *reflected appraisals*. The child lacks the equipment and experience necessary for a careful and unclouded evaluation of himself. The only guide he has is that of the significant adults who take care of him, and who treat and regard him in accordance with the way in which they have developed from their own life experience. Hence, the child experiences himself and appraises himself in terms of what the parents and others close to him manifest. By empathy, facial expression, gestures, words, deeds they convey to him the attitudes they hold toward him and their regard or lack of it for him.[1]

The child naturally accepts these attitudes as they are conveyed, because he is not yet equipped to question or to evaluate them objectively. If the significant people express a respecting, loving attitude toward him he will have a similar attitude toward himself. If, however, "they are derogatory and hateful, then he will acquire a derogatory and hateful attitude toward himself." Sullivan believes also in the ongoing formative power of subsequent experience. Nevertheless, the general prognosis is that the child will carry to the end of his days the attitudes toward himself that he learned at his mother's knee.

1. *Oedipus: Myth and Complex* (New York: Grove Press, 1955), p. 294.

The greatest fear for the shame-ridden is the fear of humiliation, which seems to spell abandonment. Humiliation causes rage. We think of Suttie's "psychic weaning" and the infant's rage in seeing the parent preferring someone, or something, else. Jung's persona is the self in its attempt to be acceptable to society. It emerges from the tension between the society-image and the unacceptable self-image much as Adler's "fiction of superiority" derives from "inferiority feeling."[2] In Otto Rank's system, both the "average man" type and the "neurotic" type fail to develop a healthy individuated will not simply because of the painfulness of "ethical guilt" but also because of an instilled conviction of shame: I can find meaning only in being bound inextricably to society (to "mother").

The shame–driven may avoid a consciousness of inner persecution by losing himself in some other identity. If this identity fails him and forces him back upon his shameful self, he can break, suicidally or psychotically. His own ego is undeveloped. It may be a mere puppet government in abject service to some expression of the outside world. In some cases this outside center may be a narcotic ring, or other demonic structure. He may be little more than id thrown on the mercy of the court of the world outside. Although weak in ego—"ego consciousness" (Adler)—he may be overridden with distorted ego ideals, the infantile reflection of his society. He tries to satisfy them under fear of abandonment. His dominant infantile hostilities may never have been curbed adequately (by guilt). Hence, he may become a man-in-rage.

Nevertheless, shame in a measure—and everyone seems to have at least a measure—can work for good. In reading the autobiographical writings of Albert Schweitzer one is struck by the recurring theme of shame. His *Memoirs of Childhood and Youth* was written after a request by his (and Freud's) friend, Oskar Pfister, the Swiss psychoanalyst-pastor. In his memoirs, Schweitzer recalls many instances of feeling acutely ashamed. When one feels ashamed, consciously, he is ashamed of some impulse or deed, or

2. See, for example, Frieda Fordham, *An Introduction to Jung's Psychology* (London: Penguin Books, 1953), p. 47.

of just being what he pictures himself to be against the backdrop of society. In John Masefield's *The Everlasting Mercy* (June, 1911), Saul Kane says after his encounter with Mrs. Jaggard: "This old mother made me see/The harm I done by being me."

The feeling of shame may be quickly caught up in the larger dynamism of guilt. Thus transformed, the emotion focuses on trying to rectify the wrong or to rationalize itself into placing the evil outside the self, whether in a victim or in circumstances or fate.

In some cases, the feeling of shame may occur at a stage of relatively positive ego development. The young child may have identified with the nurturing and generally satisfying aspects of his social environment, the good objects. His failure, whether by a fearful refusal or by want of opportunity, to introject a more threatening image, means that he has halted in the process of identification, before having to make an acute acknowledgement of any psychological separation from the social environment. Hence, he goes through life trying not to appear to that environment as the bad, unworthy kind of thing that it would surely abandon. His defenses against fear may include hostile attacks on that environment. These may be awkward cries for help, for nurturing love. Both Suttie and Horney, as we have noted, see hostility as directed anxiety.

The shame-driven individual may range in personality type from sociopath to angel of mercy. As he nears utter despair in his protests against abandonment and fatal separation, he may become bitter, antagonistic, rageful in action as well as verbal behavior. He seems to be saying to the whole world: "You have no right to abandon me! I won't let you!"

In May 1960, Caryl Chessman was executed in the gas chamber in San Quentin Prison, in California. For several years he had remained on death row. In his long maneuvering against the sentence of death he performed the laudable feat of becoming highly skilled in legal procedure. His many attempts to win freedom never included any hint of penitence or appeal for mercy. He showed no sense of guilt against society, which he addressed as though it were a kind of monolith over against himself. We can see in his situation the suggestion that shame feelings may work deeper within the unconscious than what are called specifically guilt feelings. Whatever guilt or shame there may have been was underneath the show of arrogance, pride, contempt for society, and quest for glory which this reported figure seemed to project on the screen for many viewers.

However, regardless of whether this case, or others which we could mention, can illustrate the effect of an inferiority feeling in the life of a psychopath, it does illustrate a society's official rejection of what it regards as a bad object. Yet, in a psychologically profound sense, these bad objects may be less sinful (guilty) than the society that condemns them. They have what psychoanalysts call character disorders. Theologians may regard them as at once agents and victims of "the demonic" (Tillich) and "the Kingdom of Evil" (Walter Rauschenbusch).

It seems strange that we find ourselves looking for the dynamics of shame in figures as different as Schweitzer and Chessman. Yet it is perhaps no more strange than the theory that ego ideals are determined by the emotional experience of the individual as he learns to regard this as "good" and that as "bad" in his particular social incubator. Schweitzer himself distinguished between the attitude of "world and life affirmation" and "world and life negation." They can be two different styles of life. Incidentally, Oskar Pfister says that Christ was Schweitzer's ego ideal. He thinks that Schweitzer introjected the portrait of Christ which his early societal environment provided him.[3]

Of the difference between "guilt driven" and "shame driven" types of neurosis, Gerhart Piers, in a careful study of the question, says, "Guilt-engendered activity is at best restitution (sacrifice, propitiation, atonement) which rarely frees, but brings with it resentment and frustration rage which in turn feed new guilt into the system." He contrasts with this, shame-engendered activity. It may surprise us to hear: "The shame-driven individual has better potentialities as to maturation and progress." Why? Piers goes on

---

3. *Christianity and Fear,* trans. W. H. Johnston (London: George Allen & Unwin, 1948), p. 549.

to say: "His primary identifications may be healthier to start with, his later identifications may permit him to proceed from the original images to siblings, peers, and broader aspects of the social environment. If his ambitious drive is coupled with creativeness, it may actually lead to a spontaneous curing of the original narcissistic wound."

Piers says that the "guilt-ridden person introjects and expels ('extrojects')." In contrast, the "shame-driven" person "identifies and compares." Each temperament has its peculiar hazard: "Whereas the shame driven might be propelled beyond his natural limitations and break, the guilt ridden as a rule will not even reach his potentialities."[4]

Such a comparison represents the kinds of distinctions which contemporary Freudians are seeking in their study of the ego. The shame-type of individual is marked by pre-Oedipal identifications. Adlerian man, if forced into this frame of reference, is "shame driven." However, he represents a competition-oriented culture. Indeed, as Milton Singer suggests, shame type cultures can be as industrious as guilt cultures.[5]

Erikson takes us to the crisis of early infancy in his story of Martin Luther. His "saving faith" was possible, Erikson surmises, because he retained a basic pattern of trust which was established during the earliest stage of development. This was before both shame and guilt. Nevertheless, Luther the man seems to have made his way, to some degree, past the bogs of shame and guilt. According to Erikson, he never arrived at that inner serenity which characterizes the integration of the self. But there was an abiding trust in the smiling mother image.[6] Of course we cannot validate a psychoanalytic study of Luther. However, the study as an essay on psychoanalysis as Erikson likes to apply it, sets forth a doctrine

4. Piers and Milton Singer, *Shame and Guilt* (Springfield, Ill.: Charles C. Thomas, 1953), p. 28.
5. *Ibid.*, pp. 76–79. Cf. Helen Merrell Lynd, *On Shame and the Search for Identity* (New York: Harcourt, Brace, 1958), p. 20 and *passim*. She calls attention to the distinction as it is made by Piers, and also by Franz Alexander. The distinction between guilt and shame is obscure in Freud, Max Weber, Ruth Benedict, and others.
6. *Young Man Luther* (New York: W. W. Norton & Co., Inc., 1958), pp. 265–66.

of basic trustfulness—or basic trust over mistrust—which is reminiscent of much theological writing.

The guilt driven is more inner-directed, according to much of the theory as it is applied in psychoanalysis and anthropology. However, Piers insists that shame is also essentially internalistic. Hence, we are all the more inclined to see in Alfred Adler's thought a significant corrective to Freud. Shame is felt not simply because one's nakedness (and inadequacy) is being viewed with scorn, not simply because one is being subjected to ridicule, but because an inner identification, a goal, is threatened.

Nevertheless, we distinguish between the two kinds of motivation, inward though both may be. The young Oedipus, to use the Freudian paradigm for guilt, has pitted himself against his father image for the possession of the mother image. In the process he feels as though he has lost the good father and is ever pursued by the bad father. This marked lad is impelled to restore relationship with his father, to enjoy the grace of being with the good father. He must appease the offended father. According to Freud, he does this by incorporating him, by identifying with the threatening, vengeful Laius. But, in fantasy at least, like Jacob, he has already stolen Esau's birthright. Incidentally, the Freudians have not overlooked this biblical analogue. Esau is treated as a father figure in conflict over the mother.[7] In the spirit of Suttie, we can make the appropriate criticism and suggest that here again in spite of the obviousness of it, is an expression of sibling, or Cain, jealousy. Using Suttie's frame of reference, then, we may describe guilt as a compulsion to appease the vengeful mother image in the wake of the Cain jealousy and harm to Abel. Or, to use Esau and Jacob (the younger of the two), we can say that guilt by the younger is compulsive fear of the older sibling's wrath; thus, the guilt of Jacob is analogous to that of Oedipus: the victim himself is the avenger.

The guilty one asserts himself. He acquires guilt by trying to force the outside world to conform to his values; he "loves" that society and feels beholden to it; when he sees that his bold

7. Theodor Reik, "The Wrestling of Jacob," in *Dogma and Compulsion* (New York: International Universities Press, 1951), pp. 229–51.

assertion has backfired he tries to make amends. Life was better on the other side of the offense. But the id self spoke first. The social self speaks out later, as guilt feeling.

By contrast, "Enoch walked with God. . . ."[8] Does he represent the more healthy type of shame-driven personality whose shame has been fostered by a benign, instead of evil, influence? A shame-driven person early recognizes his own inadequacy and seeks his values from the outside I—or Thou. His selfhood derives from what he early perceives in significant others around him. In Freudian terms, he can best continue with mother if he never yields to the temptation to vie with father, but chooses rather to "walk with" him.

Taking the insights of the many schools together, we conclude that the dynamism of shame should be distinguished from that of guilt. Regardless of how repressed or disguised it may be, a pervasive sense of being inferior or worthless is due to an early internalization of the privation or rejection which operates as self-degradation and self-rejection. The inner conflict is fought to a truce, characteristically, by a style of life that assumes the opposite, (superiority and glory) or else loses the self in some other self, ideal, or cause. Guilt, on the other hand, is an awareness of having offended against a relationship of reciprocal love, with the consequent danger of retaliation-in-kind. It operates as a compulsion to reconstitute the situation as it was before the offense, to undo the wrong, to make restitution.

The characteristic fear in shame is of being abandoned. The characteristic fear in guilt feeling is of being mutilated—it is a more melodramatic view of abandonment perhaps: at least this is the picture that Freudians draw for us. Both shame and guilt as conscious emotions seem to presuppose a rudimentary experience of love as reciprocal trustfulness. The dynamism of guilt includes within it that of shame, however without the degree of fixation on the shame-generating stage of development which characterizes the shame-driven person. Hence, we shall assume a working distinction between a guilty conscience and a sense of shame.

8. Gen. 5:24. Perhaps Enoch is more a symbol of the triumph of basic trustfulness.

As we do this of course we realize that the idiom has its ambiguities. For example, "I am ashamed of what I did," expresses guilt rather than shame, usually; and "I am a guilty thing!" expresses shame. Generally, we mean, therefore, that guilt relates to what I do, while shame relates to what I am. We recall Albert Ellis' description of sin, or guilt, as: (1) "I have done the wrong thing"; and (2) "I am . . . a valueless person." The first is guilt, while, the second is shame, according to our working definition.

Now, we should be ready to move on in our inquiry to the question of fear, or fearfulness, which pervades both guilt and shame feelings.

8

Pervasive Anxiety

In guilt feeling, with its "I am sorry I did that; I must make restitution!" anxiety is present with its "Something disastrous may happen!" In shame feeling the anxiety says, "Disaster awaits if I am forced back upon myself alone." The ego of self-awareness feels that it cannot endure the consequences. Guilt predicts mutilation, as well as separation. Shame predicts abandonment, "being cast into outer darkness." Both can be described as forms of separation anxiety. Indeed both may be present, as in the commonplace illustration with which we began the third chapter on the nature of guilt feelings. The father's painful "conscience" over the treatment of his small son includes feelings of unworthiness. Conscious guilt feelings often seem to be working frantically to defend the ego against some repressed, or suppressed, more dangerous sense of unworthiness. Yet we can speak of a guilt-driven as contrasted to a shame-driven type of personality. Some shame-driven individuals may seem baffling to observers who think of "conscience" as that which says, "I am responsible; I must make things right."

However, in both guilt and shame we see a dynamic factor which seems to arrive on the scene first: anxiety—uneasiness, restless fearfulness, worry. Indeed a measure of it must surely characterize every consciousness. Much has been written on the subject in recent years. The philosophy of Martin Heidegger, for instance, makes much of the concept (his is an ontology of *anxiety*: it "reveals nothingness").[1] Most essayists refer to psychologists, many to the theories of depth psychologists. Now, in our inquiry about the fall into consciousness, we shall review the concept of anxiety as it appears in various systems of psychotherapeutic theory.

1. *Was ist Metaphysik* (Frankfort: Vittorio Klostermann, 1929), p. 16. See Arne Naess, *Four Modern Philosophers*, trans. Alastair Hannay (Chicago: University of Chicago Press, 1968), p. 207.

Sigmund Freud does not restrict himself, in the long run, to but one use of the term anxiety (*Angst*). In his introductory lectures in 1916-17, he describes "normal anxiety" as the affect commonly called fear, which one has when he is acutely aware of danger. The prototype for the physical response is the affect which the infant has as he is being born. This primal separation—from the mother's body—is painful. "Neurotic anxiety" is "expectant dread" where there is not an appropriate danger apparent to the conscious mind.

In describing the "early impression . . . which is produced as a repetition in the anxiety affect," Freud briefly reviews the ordeal of birth, "the prototype for all occasions on which life is endangered, ever after to be reproduced again in us as the dread or 'anxiety' conditions." Then, like a practiced rabbi (or Christian textual exegete or classical philologist), Dr. Freud dwells on the term itself: "*Angst . . . angustiae, Enge,* a narrow place, a strait." which "accentuates the characteristic tightening in the breathing which was then the consequence of a real situation and is subsequently repeated almost invariably with an affect." It is significant that the first anxiety state was during the process of entering the world through a narrow passage. "We naturally believe that the disposition to reproduce this first anxiety condition has become so deeply ingrained in the organism, through countless generations, that no single individual can escape the anxiety affect."[2]

It may be at least suggestive to read this passage from Freud alongside the descriptions of gateways and pathways in the literature of various religions. Certainly the one in the Sermon on the Mount comes readily to mind: "Enter by the narrow gate; for the gate is wide and the way is easy, that leads to destruction, and those who enter by it are many. For the gate is narrow and the way is hard, that leads to life, and those who find it are few."[3]

---

2. Freud, *Introductory Lectures on Psycho-Analysis* (American edition: *A General Introduction to Psycho-Analysis,* trans. Joan Riviere [Garden City, N.Y.: Permabook, 1953], p. 404). Cf. *New Introductory Lectures on Psycho-Analysis,* trans. W. J. H. Sprott (New York: W. W. Norton & Co., Inc., 1933), pp. 121 f.
3. Matt. 7:13–14.

Entering the narrow way could mean facing head-on the *Angst der Kreatur*—the anxiety that one feels when he assumes the narrow way between independence and dependence? Taking the broad path could mean, especially, avoiding that anxiety which comes when one risks separation. But, in this, we are with Rank.

In a quite different figure Freud speaks also of anxiety as a signaling mechanism in the ego-dynamism which helps it mobilize resistance. Thus, one feels anxious—restless, uneasy, fearful— when the outside world, perhaps even as represented by the psychotherapist, seems to be making some demand on the ego which it is not accustomed to facing head-on. One, in effect, encounters dangers and mobilizes to meet them.

These dangers may be from within the organism, repressed drives which are pressing against the repressing ego, threatening to storm the capitol and to overthrow the government. These insurgent forces may be allied id- and superego-organized energy. The ego, we recall, evolved in order to protect the organism against "reality" when it opposed the motion of the organism. In time, Freud, speaking of ego-instincts, life instincts and *eros,* viewed the ego as the organization of these. It is much like John Dewey's "intelligence." Freud often uses "intellect" and "intelligence" almost synonomously with ego, and moves toward a kind of gospel of ego strengths. In other words, he advocates a strong central government within the personality which can withstand both id and superego unrest. The ego tries to allow the inner forces to satisfy themselves "realistically," that is, within the law of the reality principle. Like politics, the ego's practice is "the art of the possible."

At times Freud's insights seem to come close to foundering on the Oedipus complex upon which he insists, making "castration fear" *the* fear which gives force to conscience; this is a fear of mutilation. The ego, having navigated safely through the narrow waters between the Scylla of shame and the Charybdis of Oedipus guilt, then fears the anger, punishment and loss of love which are continually threatened by its *Über-ich* (the superego).

Perhaps we should digress a bit at this point to consider again the variant uses of the notion of an "over-I." This in Reinhold

Niebuhr's thought, for instance, is not at all the "superego" in Freud.[4] Another theologian, Paul Tillich, although he takes Freud seriously, repudiates his use of the term *Über-ich*.[5] Nor is the Freudian superego by any means equivalent to the transcending "self" in Percival M. Symonds' *The Ego and the Self*,[6] for yet another example. As we have seen, Freud's "I-over-I" is hostile to the "I." Nevertheless, as we have also noted, the Freudians do not discard his earlier doctrine of the "ego ideal," which is like Adler's earlier "self ideal." Many disciples do not follow Freud in his tendency to allow the earlier notion to become absorbed—or at least overshadowed—by the later concept of superego.

The Freudian superego is sadistic toward the ego. The "ego ideal," on the other hand, can be a kind of alter ego. It stands close to the ego. Indeed, it may pervade it. It may in effect be the prime minister, so complete and so early has been the ego's identification with significant adults. Perhaps the self which Symonds describes, the transcending I which Niebuhr sees, and the transcendent conscience described by Tillich, and also that which has been set forth, representatively of many theologians, by Donald Baillie[7] can be correlated better with the ego ideal than with the superego. Yet, because of the question of transcendence —does the ego ideal transcend the ego?—we must conclude that neither of the Freudian models seems to be adequate for what these philosophers and theologians regard as the self transcending itself. Of course, however, there is the Freudian doctrine of sublimation, for which Freud himself gives partial credit to his colleagues Ernest Jones, Oskar Pfister (who, we recall, was a pastor-theologian) and to his erstwhile collaborator C. G. Jung,

4. Reinhold Niebuhr, "Human Creativity and Self-Concern in Freud's Thought," in *Freud and the Twentieth Century*, ed. Benjamin Nelson (New York: Meridian, 1957), pp. 259–76.
5. I think of my conversations with Tillich and also of his *Systematic Theology*, Vol. I (Chicago: University of Chicago Press, 1951), p. 124–27.
6. New York: Appleton-Century-Crofts, 1951.
7. Especially in *Faith in God and Its Christian Consummation*, Kerr Lectures, 1926 (Edinburgh: T. and T. Clark, 1927).

who, alas, Freud thought, went off the deep end with his discovery of sublimation and substituted it for the "real."[8]

For Freud, sublimation, which has also been listed among the ego-mechanisms, is a rechanneling of raw, biological, sexual, pleasure-seeking energy. In time, it was seen by him to include also the rechanneling of destructiveness as well. But, in criticizing Jung's riding off with the doctrine, he felt that violence was done to the concept of "libido." Jung had made of it a mystical *élan vital*. Yet, in retrospect, what had Freud done for the concept and *eros* by the time he finished his tract *Civilization and Its Discontents*? Even so, although theologians may find useful the concept of a psychic (ego or "mental") "mechanism" which sublimates the biological impulses into "spiritual" or aesthetic fulfillment, they still do not seem to have from Freudian theory quite all the tools they need.

Now let us return to the theme on which we are focusing our inquiry in this chapter. Does repression create anxiety or does anxiety itself do the repressing? Incidentally, repression, according to Freud, is another one of those "mental mechanisms" by which the ego defends the organism. Freud changed his mind about the role of anxiety in repression. He came to feel that anxiety itself creates the repression, in the service, and implementation, of the ego.[9] As he tries to keep to his description of the structure of the psyche in *The Ego and the Id* (1923) Freud sees the ego as the place of fears.[10] This doctrine of course has far-reaching implications for the strategic concern with anxiety in Freudian therapy. It is largely consistent with other systems of depth psychology.

In spite of his patriarchal bias, with its focus on "castration

8. An instance of Freud's giving credit to his colleagues for this concept of sublimation is in *Group Psychology and the Analysis of the Ego,* trans. James Strachey (New York: Liveright Publishing Corp., 1951).

9. The discussion in Ernest Jones biography of Freud is helpful as we try to follow the vicissitudes in Freud's theories of anxiety. *Life and Work,* Vol. 3 (London: Hogarth, 1953), pp. 254–57.

10. See the subsequent "Female Sexuality," for instance, in *Collected Papers,* Vol. 5 (London: Hogarth, 1956), pp. 254, 266. Cf. Jung, in "Freud and Jung," *Modern Man in Search of a Soul,* Harvest Books edition (New York: Harcourt, Brace, 1933), p. 123, where he agrees with Freud that the ego is the place of fears.

fear" in the boy and "castration rage" in the girl, Freud recognized that separation anxiety is in some sense basic. After all, the occasion for the anxiety over organ inferiority (at the Oedipal stage, Freud's Sinai) is the desire for the mother. The child fears losing his loved object.[11] Like Adam and Eve in the garden he is ashamed of his nakedness; he is disturbingly aware of the fact that physically he is no match for the One who walks "alone" in the garden. This father-god is bent on mutilating him, says Freud; at least this is the individual's fantasy and the racial psyche's memory. Although Freud's views on anxiety cannot be wrenched from the various contexts in which he speaks about it, it is safe to distill this much for a correlation with other theories. Anxiety means that one is "aware" of the danger of object loss and separation.

Otto Rank, as we saw earlier, makes much of that anxiety which Freud described earlier in his introductory lectures in 1916-17. But the trauma of *Geburtstrauma* on the reading of Freud and other writings which tend to maximize anxiety in the theory of child development has caused a tightening up of definition. For example, Charles Brenner, in 1950, while addressing the New York Psychoanalytic Society, suggests, discreetly to be sure, what he calls "a minor revision" of the theory which Freud offered in *Inhibitions, Symptoms and Anxiety* (1926). According to Brenner, anxiety is an emotion or affect which the anticipation of danger evokes in the ego; as such it is not present from birth through early infancy. In the early months, the infant is aware only of pleasure and unpleasure "as far as the emotions are concerned." However, "as experience increases, and other ego functions develop" like memory and sense perception, the child learns "to predict or anticipate that a state of unpleasure (traumatic situation) will develop." He says that "the dawning ability of the child to react to danger in advance is the beginning of the specific emotion of anxiety." Anxiety is but one of the unpleasant emotions of which a person is capable. In the developing child and in

---

11. Rollo May, in *The Meaning of Anxiety* (New York: Ronald Press, 1950), pp. 112–27, sees as specially important in Freud's own views this emphasis on the fact that the child fears the loss of the mother's love by separation.

the adult, the therapist perhaps should assume that anxiety is "to become increasingly sharply differentiated from other unpleasant emotions."[12]

However, Freud himself, although he was critical of Rank's constructions upon the birth trauma, saw in it the prototype for both normal and neurotic anxiety. To be sure, he thought that there was a racial, or phylogenetic, component to the human disposition toward anxiety. Then, on top of the racially determined anxiety, specific anxieties are learned. The one which causes psychoses is likely to be some overpowering "pre-castration" fear: if during the oral phase, for instance, possibly it is the fear of being eaten or of being left to starve. If during the later infancy phase, the anal-urethral, it is possibly the fear of being flushed down the drain as nothing or as something which is despised. Melanie Klein seems true to the Freudian way of building theory when she describes basic anxiety as the fear of "extinction" by being eaten, smashed, torn to pieces, split up, especially since she elaborates her constructions with a generous use of Freud's theory of a primary death instinct, which, by the way, was formulated after his first introductory lectures.[13]

However, Freud taught that the ego cannot be genuinely occupied with a fear of death as such. It can fear only what it has experienced. It has experienced pain and separation. Klein defines "extinction" in terms of "mutilation." This seems orthodox. Since the unconscious knows not time, unassimilated past dangers are still "real" and present.

The fear of expulsion or abandonment is earlier than Oedipal fear and perhaps other fears which feature mutilation. As we have suggested earlier, mutilation fear, rejection fear, the sense of

12. Charles Brenner, "An Addendum to Freud's Theory of Anxiety," adapted from his paper (November 28, 1950), *The International Journal of Psycho-Analysis,* XXXIV, I (1953), pp. 18–24.
13. Klein, "On the Theory of Anxiety and Guilt," in *Developments in Psycho-Analysis,* ed. Joan Riviere (London: Hogarth, 1952), pp. 276, 278–79; *The Psycho-Analysis of Children,* trans. Alix Strachey (London: Leonard and Virginia Woolf at Hogarth Press, 1932), pp. 184–87, 189, 193; "The Early Development of Conscience in the Child," *Psychoanalysis Today,* ed. Sandor Lorand (New York: International Universities Press, 1944), pp. 64–74.

inferiority, awareness of privation, and the fear of extinction all may be classed as modifications of separation anxiety. This is not to say that they are not to be distinguished from each other. Indeed, such an idea as separation anxiety may be too sophisticated a construction for us to place on the earliest fears. Klein does not seem to have any problem with this kind of question, however, as she relates anxiety to the activity—and acted-out fantasy—of the child as it toys with its objects. The infant both loves and hates the mother's breast and any other object which comes its way. In fantasy he does to it everything which he then, by projection, fears it will do to him: eating, smashing, tearing to pieces. The terror is there to begin with, right in the inner world of images. Hence, the ego itself is made up of its assortment of objects. They are split into good and bad components which correspond to the two instincts which operate upon the objects as they are encountered in the outside world.

Ian Suttie tried to define anxiety in a setting more like Melanie Klein's perhaps than Karen Horney's. To be sure, his anxiety has no death instinct cause or component. Yet it is fear of the "bad mother"—the one who denies him what he wants. Incidents in this long process of psychic weaning are between the body-ego of the infant and his environing object, the mother, with whom he has been in symbiotic union. To Suttie, the love which the infant learns in his mother's lap and at her breast is a giving and taking behavior. He distinguishes it—fairly or not—from Freud's eros, which he interprets to be simply a "getting" impulse. It may be possible to correlate Suttie's "giving" impulse—love—to the activity which Klein describes as "action upon" the object by the infant as it develops musculatory awareness and control. The infant's world is busy from the very beginning, filled with fantasies of eating, tearing, smashing, and the like. There is nothing static about the psyche during the early months of life. The infant begins life acting and being acted upon, and, according to Klein, internalizing the whole business.

When we leave Freud, Klein, and Suttie for Adler and Horney, we may seem to be moving away from the infant. Even the young child seems not to be as important as he was.

To Alfred Adler, anxiety had at least two meanings. As the Ansbachers say, his use of the term was usually in describing a conscious symptom, such as phobia. He could also speak of anxiety as a device by which one tries to gain power over others. He gives an example of this in the story of a woman whose sudden "anxiety neurosis" was a means of gaining control over the activities of her husband. "But she paid for this success by very painful anxieties, so much so that her husband had been able to persuade her to come and see me," Adler writes.[14] Characteristically, he proclaims that fearfulness can be overcome "solely by that bond which binds the individual to humanity. Only that individual can go through life without anxiety who is conscious of belonging to the fellowship of man.[15]

Freud occasionally speaks of the feeling of helplessness.[16] But Adler relates the feeling of "not being able" to anxiety. The compulsive neurotic is trying to protect himself from anxiety because he has this feeling of "not being able."[17] Freud's "anxiety" is a dynamism which defends the ego—or else a dynamism by which the ego defends itself against the feeling of helplessness.

C. J. Jung sees anxiety as basically the conscious ego's reaction to the invasion of the conscious mind by irrational forces and archetypal images with which it is not prepared to cope. Jung criticizes Freud for stopping at the "question of Nicodemus." The resolution of anxiety is in a kind of new birth, by which Jung means the reconciliation of the conscious with the unconscious world, a never ending process, but one in which it is possible to make great transformational progress.[18] The ego is to the self as

14. *Problems of Neurosis: A Book of Case-Histories* (London: Kegan Paul, Trench, & Trubner, 1929), p. 154, quoted in Heinz L. and Rowena R. Ansbacher, *The Individual Psychology of Alfred Adler* (New York: Basic Books, 1956), p. 304.

15. *Understanding Human Nature,* trans. Walter Beran Wolfe (London: Allen and Unwin, 1927), p. 238; quoted by Rollo May, *The Meaning of Anxiety,* p. 134. Cf. Horney on separation anxiety.

16. Anxiety warns against the fall into helplessness. Inhibitions. See Jones, *Life and Work,* Vol. 3, pp. 255–56.

17. "Compulsion Neurosis," in *Individual Psychology,* p. 305.

18. Jung, "Freud and Jung—Contrasts," in *Modern Man in Search of a Soul,* at pp. 122–24.

the moved is to the mover in Jung's thought. The ego fears "self-sacrifice." It may be possible for us to correlate this in Jung with the death instinct theory in Freud. Of course, there is this important difference: Jung tends to believe—more hopefully—in the forces within, which try to move the ego to sacrifice. It may be illuminating to us to ponder some of Jung's illustrations of this doctrine. We have mentioned the encounter of Nicodemus with Jesus and the prescription "You must be born again."[19] Jung thinks that the story of Abraham's near sacrifice of Isaac and Jesus' agony in Gethsemane and subsequent crucifixion illustrate the self-ego (mover-moved) dynamics. "Fear of self-sacrifice lurks deep in every ego, and this fear is often only the precariously controlled demand of the unconscious forces to burst out in full strength."[20]

Jung's idea of unconscious pressure upon the conscious, and "fear" as the precarious control over this demand suggests a continued, if modified, adherence to the old Freudian (and pre-Freudian) psychodynamics.[21] Anxiety is emotion felt by the executive conscious ego when the unconscious world theatens to storm the palace. The energy of anxiety is that pressure upon the gates. But, with Jung, the unconscious may well be bringing salvation. We are at once aware of the difficulties and perhaps the perceptiveness in Jung's way with the self as it is to be distinguished from the ego and with *Angst* as it is seen in dynamic relation to the two. In religious sacrifice the self sacrifices the ego to the larger reality.[22] Anxiety, for Jung, is the ego's "fear of the dominants of the collective unconscious," the individual's reaction to the invasion of his conscious.[23]

---

19. John 3.
20. Jung, *Psychology and Religion: West and East,* Bollingen Series xx, vol. 11 (New York: Bollingen Foundation, 1954), p. 521. Also, "The Sequence of the Transformation Rite," *ibid.,* pp. 208–96.
21. Cf. Henri F. Ellenberger, *The Discovery of the Unconscious: The History and Evolution of Dynamic Psychiatry,* chaps. 3–6, 7, 9 (New York: Basic Books, 1970).
22. Jung, *ibid.,* pp. 261 f.
23. Rollo May, citing H. Goodwin Watson's formulation of Jung's concepts, *The Meaning of Anxiety,* pp. 136–37.

Karen Horney distinguishes what she calls "basic anxiety" from what is yet more basic, the *Angst der Kreatur,* one's natural dread before the obvious power and mystery of nature and the *other.* Even this anxiety, with its suggestion of dependence and the danger of being removed from that upon which one depends, may be regarded as a kind of separation anxiety. To be sure it is somehow more than that.[24]

Paul Tillich, in *The Courage to Be,* is depth psychologically perceptive, especially as he discusses this theme. He says anxiety is the "threat of non-being." Indeed some psychotherapists have simply adopted this theologian's formulation.[25]

Horney's essays on anxiety were not ignored by the theologians of anxiety, notably Tillich and Reinhold Niebuhr, yet both men failed to do her justice on the matter of anxiety. In his Gifford lectures, Niebuhr takes time to contrast his own conception of anxiety to that of Karen Horney. But Mary Frances Thelen is probably right in her judgment that Niebuhr misconstrued what Horney was saying. At any rate he was too categorical in his comparison. This is not to deny the perceptiveness of Niebuhr's own contribution as a theologian in the interpretation of anxiety as "the temptation to sin."[26]

Once, in conversation with me, Tillich dismissed Horney's "basic anxiety" as not being "basic." He was a personal friend of the psychoanalyst, and he conducted her funeral, in 1952. However, he regarded her definitions of anxiety as failing to distinguish properly between "normal"—or what he called "existential" anxiety—and "neurotic" anxiety. For Tillich, the fear of non-being was, of course, the basic anxiety. Niebuhr's complaint was that

---

24. Horney, *The Neurotic Personality of our Time* (New York: W. W. Norton & Co., Inc., 1937), pp. 94–95.
25. Hanna Colm, "Healing as Participation," *Psychiatry,* XVI (1953), and the by now famous R. D. Laing, "An Examination of Tillich's Theory of Anxiety and Neurosis," *British Journal of Medical Psychology,* XXX, pt. 2 (1951), pp. 88–91.
26. *Man As Sinner in Contemporary American Realistic Theology* (New York: King's Crown, 1946), p. 185. See Niebuhr, *The Nature and Destiny of Man,* Vol. 1 (New York: Charles Scribner's Sons, 1955), p. 44n and p. 192 for his references to Horney.

Horney limited anxiety to sociological causality and significance. This resembles the Freudian critique of Horney and all revisionists that leave the somatic moorings for the social.

However, in defense of Horney's thesis, we have to recognize that she distinguished between "basic" *Angst* and what she called the "basic anxiety" of neurosis. This separation anxiety which underlies neurosis is, in its incipiency, a wound to the spirit of the young child, or infant. It is not a once-and-for-all experience, but a pattern which is shaped by middle childhood. The "basic anxiety" is repressed. "The more unbearable the anxiety the more thorough the protective means have to be." Horney's views on this are like those of present-day Freudian ego-psychologists. The threat to the ego's defenses is the underlying anxiety and basic hostility which it generates. The basic anxiety is fear that the world is hostile. Anxiety is at once a frantic denial of this kind of conclusion and a resistance to it.[27] In other words, anxiety can be construed as a way of hoping.

With Erikson, also with Suttie, Sullivan, and many others, Horney teaches that the question is not Hamlet's "To be or not to be" so much as it is "To trust or not to trust." Is the world basically trustworthy or untrustworthy? is the infant's existential and practical question.

Horney recognizes the drive for superiority which Adler makes the dynamism for all neurosis. But she sees it as one of two dominant patterns, the other being the craving for affection. Indeed, like Suttie, she says the underlying drive is for affection, even though the life style may seem to be a loud denial of any such interest. Suttie, in offering a corrective to Adler, says: "Instead of seeking other peoples' love for the sake of power it confers upon us of getting them to do things for us . . . it often comes to be the other way about. We get them to do things, perhaps needless things, for us in order to be assured of their love."[28]

For Horney, as with other theorists we have associated with her, the basic anxiety asks: "Am I loved?" It does not begin as

27. Horney, *The Neurotic Personality*, p. 89. Other references for this treatment of Horney's views: *Ibid.*, pp. 9, 96, 95–100, 105.
28. *The Origins of Love and Hate* (London: Kegan Paul, 1935), p. 49.

for Adler, with the conviction: "I am deficient." No, the sequence of convictions is rather: "I am not loved; therefore I must be deficient." The neurotic is like a drowning man in his preoccupation with being an acceptable self. This preoccupation, along with the dammed-up hostility, accounts for the neurotic's characteristic "disregard of the other's personality, peculiarities, limitations, needs, wishes, developments."[29] Because of his own deficiency of love he cannot love his neighbor as he loves himself. He hates him*self*, blaming himself for the primal rejection and cumulative pattern of rejection which something about it seems to invite. He seeks for himself and for the view of others another face and presence, a goodness which he can never find. He is hard on himself; he is hard on others.

Melanie Klein believes that a child can be helped to overcome his fear of being destroyed (rejected). What she recommends is a kind of love—we may even call it *agape*—therapy. We recall how she and Rank were influenced by Ferenczi, as were many others. Ferenczi stressed the therapist's role as "loving parent" before the resolution of what are called the transference (and counter-transference) crises during therapy. As Klein puts it, recommending that the insight be programmed into our nurture and education of the child, the child can be placed under the sway of his life-and-love instincts if the environment tips the scales in favor of them instead of the "death instincts."

Horney tries to make a distinction between "normal" and "neurotic," but she leaves one guessing as to whether there can be any qualitative distinction. Everyone seems to be more or less neurotic. In Klein's system there is no such problem; since patterns of trust and mistrust are woven by a dynamic interplay between the organism and its objects, hostility seems to come from within the psyche itself. Of course, this may be easily vitiated further by too much outside hostility. True, she tends to reify emotions. However, if the reader tries to get behind the sometimes grotesque, often Vedic, use of "objects," he can gain fresh insight. She says: "The analysis of small children between two-and-a-half

29. Horney, *The Neurotic Personality,* pp. 110 f.

and five years clearly shows that for all children in the beginning external reality is mainly a mirror of the child's own instinctual life." She goes on to say that if she were asked to give a brief generalization for the psychoses, she would say "that the main groupings correspond to defenses against the main developmental phases of sadism."[30] When she refers to sadism she is trying to direct the reader's attention to infantile patterns of exercising oneself upon the objects of his environment in a destructive manner, which in turn corresponds to that which he experiences as the environment's acting upon himself. The infant is born "with a chip on his shoulder." But he also wears a smile quite soon after that trauma of birth. It is possible for us to blend Klein's constructions with the idea of *Angst der Kreatur*. Certainly, she is not restricting her elementary definitions (descriptions) to "abnormal" as distinguished from "normal." The psychoses of adolescents and adults hark back to normative "psychoses" in infancy. These are, among other things, anxiety states.

Klein's infant comes into the world crying for oxygen. He needs warmth like that he experienced inside the womb. As he develops, each area of his appetite needs satisfaction, including the natural drive to exercise his muscles, which he in effect exercises "against." Naturally he meets resistance, negation, hence, "evil." Anxiety is the fear of the bad object. It is both external and internalized. Also, we may say, anxiety is generally the fear one has of the trouble he gets into by "just doing what comes naturally." Hostility, for Klein, is both the exercising against objects and the projection of the fears.

We recall the work of W. Ronald Fairbairn, who developed his theories in dialogue with Klein. Henry Guntrip, a student of Fairbairn, in an essay on anxiety, seems to support the construction we have offered here. Of course, like his teacher, Guntrip chooses not to personify—or anthropomorphize—instincts in the manner

---

30. Klein, "The Psychotherapy of the Psychoses," reprinted in *Contributions to Psycho-Analysis, 1921–1941* (London: Hogarth, 1948), p. 251. See also her "The Oedipus Complex in the Light of Early Anxieties," *ibid.*, pp. 339–90.

of Klein. Like Fairbairn he stresses the object-ego encounter.[31]

It is interesting that Klein makes the life forces dominant. She offers a corrective to the easily pessimistic tendency of Freud's theory of a death instinct. True, "the death instinct (destruction impulses) is the primary factor in the causation of anxiety." But healthy weaning and education result in mitigation of aggression. "Anxiety arising from the perpetual activity of the death instinct, though never eliminated, is counteracted and kept at bay by the power of the life instinct."[32] Freud's idea of salvation by sublimation is reminiscent of Schopenhauer's doctrine of contemplation as the way "out of" or, perhaps, more fairly, "through," this existence.[33]

Otto Rank also rejects the logic of pessimism. He says that his own thought was to Freud's negative voluntarism as was Nietzsche's to Schopenhauer's and to that which Rank sees as Old Testament negative voluntarism. Rank takes care to distinguish his concept of will from that of Nietzsche as well, however.[34] We recall that he defines genuine guilt as "ethical guilt." Moreover Rank was drawn to an *agape*istic ethic.

To him, the basic anxiety is modulated into two forms of fear, what he calls "death fear" and "life fear." This primal ambivalent fear "is derived on the one side from the experience of the individual as a part of the whole, which is then separated from it and obliged to live alone (birth); on the other side, from the final necessity of giving up the hard won wholeness of individuality." This necessity of self-loss as individuality-loss is death itself. Unlike Freud, Rank can conceive of a genuine fear of death.

---

31. *Psychotherapy and Religion,* pt. 1 (New York: Harper & Row, 1957), pp. 17–88.

32. "On the Theory of Anxiety and Guilt," in *Developments in Psycho-Analysis,* p. 291.

33. See Freud, "The Libido Theory," in *Collected Papers,* Vol. 5, pp. 132–33. Cf. his *A General Introducton,* p. 354, 384–85; *New Introductory Lectures,* pp. 132–34; *An Outline,* trans. James Strachey (New York: W. W. Norton & Co., Inc., 1949), pp. 31–32 and *passim.* Also cf. his "On Narcissism," *Collected Papers,* Vol. 4, pp. 151–52.

34. Rank, *Truth and Reality,* in *Will Therapy and Truth and Reality,* trans. Jessie Taft (New York: Alfred A. Knopf, 1945), pp. 226–27.

Melanie Klein also conceives of a genuine "death fear," the "fear of extinction," as we have noted. In speaking of such a fear, Guntrip modulates it into that anxiety "which is our reaction in the face of any threat of destruction of the possibility of good-object relationships, either by the destruction of ourselves or of our love-objects and the experiencing of the loss of good-objects coupled with being left at the mercy of inescapable bondage to persecuting bad-objects."[35]

In speaking of a genuine fear of death, Rank goes on to say: "This universal human primal fear which varies only in accordance with life age and difference of sex, seems to lead to two different life forms which are conditioned by the manner in which the individual can solve this part-whole problem."[36]

Rank's concern for individuation corresponds somewhat with Horney's for the "real self." His appreciation for the fear of individuation seems to be larger in dimension than either Adler's idea of basic inferiority feeling or Horney's concept of basic anxiety. Yet her hypothesis of a neurotic displacement of the "real self" by idealized self-images or the "ideal self" because of rejection feeling seems consonant enough with Rank's doctrine of "average man" type, "neurotic" type, and "artist" type. The "average man" settles for a perhaps more realistic but nevertheless "ideal" self-image, namely, that which is merely the reflection of the countenance of society. He surrenders his selfhood to his particular society. The "neurotic" tries ever frantically to identify with some impossible "ideal self" imposed upon him by early experience which denies to him both wholeness and individuation. The "artist" accepts the challenge of his "real self" at all costs, and not without anxiety! He fears the loss of society and the loss of his real self. But he takes the risk and lives "creatively," ever mindful of the risk which life is—with death inevitably out there waiting.

Harry Stack Sullivan, who is noted for his relative success in work with schizophrenics, seems to have held his theories always

35. Guntrip, *Psychotherapy and Religion,* pp. 41 f.
36. *Will Therapy,* p. 134.

close to his clinical method. He tried to avoid too elaborate a "metapsychology." Although he was influenced by Freud, he purposely chose his own vocabulary, as we have noticed. To Sullivan, "anxiety" is a term which simply denotes "apprehension of danger." In neurosis it is apprehension of disapproval in interpersonal relations. We recall that to Sullivan the "personality" is actually an interpersonal phenomenon. Anxiety arises out of the infant's apprehension of disapproval by "significant persons" in his interpersonal world.[37]

Sullivan's special contribution to the topic of anxiety is his emphasis on its effect on awareness itself. Security, based on non-separation from the personal environment, is the driving concern of the developing "waking self" within the "self system." The anxiety of infancy and early childhood both shapes the "self" of the "self system" and sets the pattern for its attentiveness and its "selective inattention."[38]

Frieda Fromm-Reichmann, a colleague of Sullivan, speaks of the "fear of psychological death," and correlates it with Paul Tillich's fear of "non-being" and Kurt Goldstein's fear of nothingness.[39]

Oskar Pfister was in a unique position within the Freudian larger circle. His correspondence with Freud has been published as *Psychoanalysis and Faith*. Pfister wrote a thick volume on anxiety,[40] in which he wears both hats as he presents his thesis on

---

37. "Anxiety is related to the loss of esteem for one by oneself or by others." (Patrick Mullahy, "The Theories of Harry Stack Sullivan" in *The Contributions of Harry Stack Sullivan* [New York: Hermitage House, 1952–53], p. 33.)

38. We follow Rollo May on Sullivan, *The Meaning of Anxiety*, pp. 149–50. Selective inattention is analogous to disavowal among the Freudian mechanisms.

39. Fromm-Reichmann refers to Tillich's *The Courage to Be* (New Haven: Yale University Press, 1952) and to Goldstein's *Human Nature in the Light of Psychopathology* (Cambridge, Mass: Harvard University Press, 1940) and *The Organism* (New York: American Book, 1939).—"Psychiatric Aspects of Anxiety," in *An Outline of Psychoanalysis*, Clara Thompson, et al., eds. (New York: Random House, The Modern Library, 1955), pp. 113–36.

40. *Christianity and Fear*, trans. W. H. Johnston (London: George Allen & Unwin, 1948). At one time Pfister was offered a chair in theology at the

what he regards as the essence of Christian "gospel." Two notable differences with Freud allow him to venture an original psycho-analytic theory of anxiety and its meaning in the history of religion and culture. Pfister modifies the libido theory, refusing to go along at all on the later theory of instinctual dualism, and he holds to an earlier theory of anxiety.

As we have seen in the early part of this chapter, Freud once regarded anxiety as produced by repression. It was transformed libido or aim-inhibited erotic energy which pressed against the ego, like water against a dam. He later chose to regard anxiety as a kind of signaling system within the ego (that is, within the dam itself). It is not the repressed but the represser, and in its work of repressing it alerts the ego to danger.[41] Pfister prefers to stay with the notion of anxiety as dammed-up energy pressing against the executive self. Then, he reconstructs *eros.* He tries to broaden the meaning of *eros (die Liebe)* to include that which he thinks Plato meant by the term. Freud himself, in *Group Psychology and the Analysis of the Ego,* argues that Plato, and indeed even the Apostle Paul, meant pretty much what he does by their word "love."[42] However, what Pfister calls love Freud calls "tender feeling" which is derived from sexuality—it is sublimated sexual,

---

University of Zurich. He kept up a running debate with Freud regarding the nature and uses of religion. See, besides the correspondence, Ernest Jones, *The Life and Work,* 2 vols., *passim.* Freud tolerated Pfister's role as a clergyman, but he professed not to be able to share his view of "the sublimation" Freud called "religious." After Pfister wrote a book on psycho-analysis applied to education (*Was beitet die Psychoanalyse dem Erzieher* [Leipzig: 1917]) Freud wrote him, beginning with a bit of praise and then saying," I am dissatisfied with one point: your contradiction of my sexual theory and my ethics. I grant you the latter. . . . If we must speak of ethics I admit to having a high ideal, from which most people I know sadly deviate." Then in a lucid paragraph Freud defends his component-instincts theory against any attempt to think of libido without correlating it to the "erotogenic zones." (Quoted in Jones, *Life and Work,* Vol. 2, pp. 457 f.)

41. Compare *A General Introduction to Psycho-Analysis,* First Introductory Lectures, p. 418, in 1915–17, with *New Introductory Lectures,* pp. 121 f., in 1933.

42. "wie Nachmansohn und Pfister in Einzelnen dargelegt haben." (*Mas-senpsychologie und Ich-Analyse* [Leipzig: International Psychoanalytischer Verlag, 1921], p. 43.) Freud is referring especially to Oskar Pfister, "Plato: a Fore-Runner of Psycho-Analysis," *The International Journal of Psycho-Analysis,* III (1922). See *Group Psychology,* pp. 38–39.

biologically sexual, love, "aim-inhibited sexuality." Nevertheless Pfister stubbornly held on to his own construct. He remained faithful by agreeing that it comes under the rubric "sublimation."

Pfister places the psychoanalytic concept of *Angst* into the New Testament Johannine context: "There is no fear (*phobos*) in love (*agape*); but perfect love casts out fear. For fear has to do with punishment, and he who fears is not perfected in love."[43] The two chief causes of anxiety are: (1) an interference with "the impulse toward love in general," and (2) "a sense of guilt (a special form of this interference) in particular." Logically, then, if guilt is a cause of anxiety, Pfister *seems* to be arguing against our thinking of guilt feeling as a composite emotion, including anxiety.

The offenses against humanity due to anxiety as it has tried to lose itself in hostility have resulted primarily from the damming up of "primary, moral or of religious love as well as inhibitions of self-love, love of others, and love of God."[44]

As Pfister sees it, love is the dominant component in guilt feeling. Christian love—*agape*—is the proper answer to guilt and the anxiety in it. Such love, to Pfister, includes "reverence." But it is not in the radical contrast suggested by Anders Nygren in *Agape and Eros*. Pfister finds Emil Brunner's *Eros und Liebe* more helpful to his thesis.[45] Whatever fault there is "does not lie with original Christianity," he says, "but in its neuroticization at the hands of neurotic Christians, whether theologians, clerics or laymen, and in the de-sublimation which occurred even when neuroses were absent." Through the centuries, crimes in the name of Christianity, including Geneva's burning of Servetus, have been committed by way of defenses against the free-flowing love which has been dammed up in psyche and society by erroneous dogma about the wrath of God. Dogmas tend to hold back love and to defeat "the gospel."[46]

---

43. I John 4:18, as quoted in *Christianity and Fear*, p. 46.
44. Pfister, *ibid.*, p. 52.
45. *Ibid.*, pp. 515–18.
46. *Ibid.*, pp. 574–75; pp. 210–15, 268–69, 453–54, p. 572 and *passim*.

Another Freudian, Theodor Reik, has written a commentary on the phenomenon of dogma. According to Reik, "dogma," as rigid, propositional adherence to religious symbols, is a compulsive effort to overcome religious doubt. "It is a reaction phenomenon, a means of repressing impulses of filial rebellion and revolution and a compromise formation for their repression and fusion with veneration and love."[47] Reik's doctrine is more consistent than Pfister's with Freud's own "etiology" of religious phenomena.

Despite the buoyancy of Pfister's work, the term *Angst,* does at times become elusive of precise definition. Generally, it seems to mean fear of danger, especially from within because of an erroneous conviction about reality. Hence, the anxious ego is aware of the reality of neurotic hostility in the world and of hostility in general. It is governed by such neurotic realism. But the healthy ego should be aware of the reality of pervasive love—"the love of Christ"—in the world and thus be governed by that reality. The ego should be free to allow the id forces of love to express themselves. The individual should assume a freedom like that of the paragon of ego-strength and outgoing love, Jesus. Thus, Pfister, while using a Freudian frame of reference, speaks nonetheless as a liberal Christian pastor. Man is by nature good and genuinely loving toward his fellow men. It is his acculturation that has made him fearful and hostile toward others.

Why, then, does society fall short of complete freedom to allow love to express itself? Freud himself would respond to the question by restricting the id energy of *eros* (love) to: (1) desire for pleasure from objects (*Objektbesetzung*—object-cathexis—and object-appropriating are as natural as hunger is food-consuming), and (2) the desire which is sometimes fused with deathfulness, that organization of counter-instincts which destroy the interests of lifefulness.[48]

---

47. *Dogma and Compulsion* (New York: International Universities Press, 1951), pp. 56–57.
48. Hatred is prior to "tender feeling." ("Instincts and Their Vicissitudes," [1915] *Collected Papers,* Vol. 4, pp. 60–83, and *An Outline* [1940], pp. 19–24.) In *An Outline* (p. 20) and in *Civilization and its Discontents* (*passim*) Freud seems to move, if ever so slightly, away from his mechanistic model of eros. The aim of eros is "to bind together."

Both the Freudian Pfister and the independent Ian Suttie consider anxiety to be the source of hostility. Along with Karen Horney and others they see the polarity of good and evil as essentially that of love and fear. Fear can take the form of hate. This conviction is expressed forcefully, if not completely convincingly, in Pfister's discourse on anxiety and Christianity.

Erich Fromm, a revisionist like Horney, also emphasizes the cultural determination of anxiety. Like Otto Rank, he calls for courage to become individuated in responsible relationship. *Escape from Freedom, Man for Himself,* and *The Sane Society* all deal with the theme, as do later works, including *The Art of Loving,* where he says: "The awareness of human separation, without reunion by love—is the source of shame. It is at the same time the source of guilt and anxiety."

Fromm, along with several others, including O. Hobart Mowrer and Paul Tillich, is discussed in Rollo May's *The Meaning of Anxiety.* Quite recently, May has addressed himself to what he considers the dominant malaise of the late 1960's—his title gives the clue: *Love and Will.* But, in the late 1940's, the dominant distress seemed to him to be anxiety. "The quantity of anxiety prevalent in the present period arises from the fact that the assumptions underlying modern culture are themselves threatened." In saying this, May is following the lead of Karl Mannheim and Abram Kardiner.[49]

Although he believes that normal anxiety should be distinguished from neurotic anxiety, May defines anxiety generally as apprehension aroused by a threat to some value one holds essential to his existence "as a personality." Normal anxiety is this existential anxiety. It is difficult to imagine anyone living who is free of it.[50]

In another book, May says: "Anxiety is the human being's basic reaction to a danger to his existence or to some value he identifies with his existence."[51] This statement reflects the empha-

49. *The Meaning of Anxiety,* p. 188.
50. *Ibid.,* p. 227.
51. *Man's Search for Himself* (New York: W. W. Norton & Co., Inc., 1953), p. 40.

sis which May and others share with the existential analysis of Ludwig Binswanger.

Although he was a respected member of the International Association of Psychoanalysts and a friend of Freud from the early years of the movement, the Swiss psychiatrist Binswanger was able to blaze a trail of his own. There were few who could do that and continue, at the same time, in the good graces of Freud.[52] From their first acquaintance they respected each other's originality without expecting too much in the way of that type of agreement which is essentially compliance.[53]

In some respects Binswanger's approach to therapy parallels that of others, including American theorists, notably Harry Stack Sullivan. However, Binswanger was more in touch with currents in philosophy, being influenced most by the kind of existentialism propounded by Martin Heidegger and Karl Jaspers (who himself was for a time a psychiatrist, and incidentally, quite critical of Freudianism) after Søren Kierkegaard.

Binswanger speaks of the patient's *Umwelt, Mitwelt,* and *Eigenwelt.* In time, he largely replaces these categories with "existential modes" reflecting the *dasein* of Heidegger. These are: (1) dual, which is somewhat like Sullivan's "need for intimacy" in interpersonal relations and like the intimacy crisis and need in Erikson, and much like the I-Thou relationship which Martin Buber considers as basic, (2) plural, which is the consciousness of being one among many, with the resultant patterns of competitiveness, and (3) anonymous, which is characterized by broken identity, depersonalization trends, and the like.[54]

This movement in depth psychology derives from both pre-Freudian Swiss psychiatry and Freudian psychology, as well as existentialism. Existential analysts consider the therapist's task as three-fold: (1) to investigate the entire structure of the patient's existence in order to help him determine its basic meaning and direction, (2) to understand the various worlds in which he lives,

52. May et al., eds., *Existence* (New York: Basic Books, 1958), pp. 48, 121 f.
53. Jones, *Life and Work,* Vol. 2, p. 128; Vol. 3, p. 170.
54. *Existence, loc. cit.*

and (3) to give him the biographical kind of psychoanalysis which the Freudians stress.[55]

We recall William James' analysis of the "why" of religious institutions: "The warring gods and formulas of the various religions do indeed cancel each other, but there is a certain uniform deliverance in which religions appear to meet." It consists of two parts: the problem and the solution. The problem is "an uneasiness—a sense that there is something wrong about us as we naturally stand."[56] Perhaps this is just as true of the warring systems of psychotherapy.

By the time our inquiry, beginning with Freud, comes to the existential analysts, and harks back to William James, we find ourselves perhaps simply reiterating the kind of description we find in Augustine: "Our hearts are restless till they find their rest . . ."[57] and in John Calvin, who, looking within, sees an "inner world of misery."[58]

Existential fear is like Tillich's "fear of non-being." It is like that awareness which Joseph Haroutunian, a Presbyterian theologian, expresses:

> I was born. I was not, and then I was. I am, but I was not. I am, but I shall not be. Having not been, I am; I am coming not to be what I was; I am coming not to be; I virtually am not. I was not, and I shall not be. I am as he who was not and shall not be. Therefore, I act necessarily not as I-am-and-ever-shall-be, but as I-am-and-was-not-and-shall-not-be.[59]

Extrapolating from case studies, Rollo May theorizes that "neurotic anxiety" arises not from rejection alone, but from rejection in contradiction to expectations. Subjects who experienced

55. *Loc. cit.* For a critical appraisal of the system see Ford and Urban, *Systems of Psychotherapy* (New York: John Wiley and Sons, Inc., 1963), pp. 445–80.

56. William James, *The Varieties of Religious Experience,* Gifford Lectures (New York: Random House, The Modern Library, 1929), pp. 497–98.

57. *Confessions,* I, 1. "In Thee" completes the statement.

58. *Institutes of the Christian Religion,* trans. Henry Beveridge (Grand Rapids: William B. Eerdmans Pub. Co., 1953), I, 1, Vol. 1.

59. *The Lust for Power* (New York: Charles Scribner's Sons, 1949), pp. 50–1.

unmistakably rejection by their parental environment, have been known to be relatively free from neurotic anxiety. Victims of such anxiety are likely to be persons who feel rejected but for some reason continue to expect to be accepted.[60] In other words, while there is anxiety there is hope.

Søren Kierkegaard and Reinhold Niebuhr have spoken of anxiety as temptation, the dizziness of freedom. The opportunity is to take or to avoid the "narrow gate." It may be appropriate to construe guilt and shame as ways of approaching and avoiding that gate.

Anxiety presupposes hope, even as guilt presupposes love, and shame presupposes trust. However, we discern the presence of anxiety in both guilt and shame. The sense of guilt is complicated by underlying shame and mistrust. Depending on how we define it, anxiety may antedate both guilt and shame.

If there has been little or no experience of the trustworthiness necessary for the human infant to grow on, then it is doubtful that he can even confront the "strait gate" and set foot upon the "narrow path" that leads to the kind of life which both psychotherapists and theologians are wont to envision. He can hardly move beyond being anxious about what he will eat and what he will put on. How can he be concerned for "the Kingdom of God" or for something like individuated life in community?

60. *The Meaning of Anxiety,* pp. 235–55, especially p. 243. Cf. Seward Hiltner and Karl Menninger, eds., *Constructive Aspects of Anxiety* (Nashville: Abingdon Press, 1963).

9

When Hope Is Gone

While anxiety is that restlessness of spirit which says, "Something disastrous may happen," despair is the conviction that "something disastrous has happened!" Guilt, fallen into despair, says, "No restitution is possible." Shame, when lost in despair, says, "There is no worth in me, nothing for me, with me or around me." Despair is hopelessness. It is the triumph of distrust. Even anxiety is gone.

Søren Kierkegaard had much to say about sin, anxiety, and despair. In fact, he defined sin as despair, the guilt before God. "Sin is this: before God, or with the conception of God, to be in despair at not willing to be oneself, or in despair at willing to be oneself."[1] We have already seen how such thinking has influenced the depth psychology of our time, notably Otto Rank and Ludwig Binswanger. Kierkegaard defines as "sin" both the life fear and the death fear (Rank) if they, either of them, go so far as to rule out the opportuntiy which is signalled by the other. One faces the human limitations of either direction as he tries to realize himself as a person. The despair "of weakness" refuses the risk of becoming separate; that is, it refuses to accept the separateness required for individuation. This is the Kierkegaardian theme which Rank elaborates. The despair "of strength" is a defiant willingness to be individuated to the extent of denying dependence, interdependence, relationship. This suggests the despair which the Adlerian man of "a neurotic style of life" may well illustrate.

One aspect of anxiety says, "I risk being separated." The despair which refuses to risk becoming independent or individuated, says, "I am destroyed if I am separated; therefore I cannot be separated." The anxiety says, "I am dependent, although I am being forced to assume independence." The despair says, "If I

1. *The Sickness Unto Death,* in *Fear and Trembling and The Sickness Unto Death,* trans. Walter Lowrie (New York: Anchor Books, 1954), p. 208.

assume independence, I am completely stranded; being thrown on my own I am nothing. There is nothing in me to contain, nothing upon which to rely." Despair is the painful affirmation of nothingness—or acquiescence in a kind of nihilism. The other face of anxiety says, "I must become myself, individuated, or I will be swallowed up, lost, put out of control like an aircraft without a pilot." The despair says, "Any softness toward others or toward the importuning of community-feeling or the claims of existing in relationship means being swallowed up, lost, put out of control." Hopelessness can destroy both individuation potential and community potential.

The clinical terms which suggest despair include "depression" and "depression state." Melanie Klein makes depression state pivotal in the formation of the ego-superego structure of the individual. The infant's nodal anxiety is like that which is seen in the depressive syndromes of both psychosis and neurosis. It is superimposed on both paranoid and schizoid characteristics. The paranoid depression is a kind of despairing sense of persecution by the bad objects which have been internalized during the first few months of life. Klein adopts W. Ronald Fairbairn's conclusions as to the primacy of a schizoid stage, in which objects are split.[2] The depression state is that in which the evil seems to be victorious over the good, or, in Klein's system, the death instincts threaten supremacy over the life instincts. Hence, depression is anxiety nearing despair. She calls the depression state central in the development of the infant.[3]

Klein goes on to say that "the fluctuations between the depressive and the manic position are an essential part of normal development." Depressive anxieties are fear that the loved objects and that the self may be destroyed. The ego is driven by these anxieties "to build up omnipotent and violent fantasies, partly for the purpose of controlling and mastering the 'bad,' dangerous objects,

2. Fairbairn, *Psychoanalytic Studies of the Personality* (London: Tavistock, 1952). Klein, "Notes on Some Schizoid Mechanisms," in *Developments in Psycho-Analysis,* ed. Joan Riviere (London: Hogarth, 1952), pp. 292–320.
3. Klein, "A Contribution to the Psycho-genesis of Manic-Depressive States," *Ibid.,* pp. 282–310. Cf. Klein, *Envy and Gratitude* (New York: Basic Books, 1957).

partly in order to save and restore the loved ones." Both destructive and reparative fantasies of omnipotence are "at work from the beginning and pervade the life of the infant." Also, "part of the death instinct which is retained in the ego causes aggression to be turned against" the object which persecutes it. According to her construction, life and death drives (correlated with musculatory behavior)—interacting—govern the whole of mental life.[4]

In dealing with the subject of despair, Karen Horney looks for insight in philosophy, if not theology. She draws upon Kierkegaard and John Macmurray as she states that despair is fundamentally "at being ourselves." The only true significance possible to our existence is "to be ourselves fully and completely."[5]

Horney describes "hopelessness" as the painful failure to realize this significance. Despair then is "an ultimate product of unresolved conflicts." She depicts an inner war between contrary impulses and the self-image. There is no victory for the will to become one's true self. With Kierkegaard she describes the man who may seem to function normally although he really is in despair.[6]

One pattern which despair takes is what Horney describes as "resignation." Another pattern is what Horney describes under the rubric of "destructiveness." As we have noted, she feels that both the classical and the later Freudian theories of instincts are inadequate for explaining this phenomenon. Destructiveness is a pattern which grows out of societal influences which are experienced as rejection. The destructive person has been deprived of a healthy, objective appreciation for himself. Varieties of despair as it produces sadistic "trends" are: striving to enslave others, to

---

4. "Mourning and Its Relation to Manic-Depressive States," in *Contribution to Psycho-Analysis, 1921–1941* (London: Hogarth, 1948), p. 316, and see "on the Development of Mental Functioning," *International Journal of Psycho-Analysis,* XXIX (1958), p. 85, an article in which she is trying to communicate her insights to her colleagues (but rivals) among the ego-psychologists; and "Some Theoretical Conclusions Regarding the Emotional Life of the Infant," in *Developments in Psycho-Analysis,* pp. 198–236.
5. Macmurray, *Reason and Emotion* (London: Faber & Faber, 1935), quoted in Horney, *Our Inner Conflicts* (New York: W. W. Norton & Co., Inc., 1946), p. 183.
6. *Ibid.,* p. 185.

play on or with the emotions of others, to exploit, to frustrate others, to disparage or humiliate others.

The despairing, destructive person, according to Horney, is one who has been overcome by the feeling of being left out, forever excluded, defeated, and at the same time, not able to become resigned. "Hence he starts to hate life and all that is positive in it. But he hates it with the burning envy of one who is withheld from something he ardently desires. It is the bitter, begrudging envy of a person who feels that life is passing him by."[7] Horney relates hopelessness to Nietzsche's *Lebensneid*. The destructive man-in-despair is trying to realize himself destructively through others. He has nothing to lose; he reasons that he can only gain by being destructive, according to a desperate logic.

Rarely, however, do sadistic tendencies characterize the total outward personality. They can be mixed with manifestations of the inner fear of their destructiveness. The Freudian idea of an ego mechanism of reaction-formation may help us understand what is going on. Sadistic impulses can be so repressed that the person may lean over backward to avoid frustrating others.

In her book, *Neurosis and Human Growth,* Horney speaks of self-hate and self-contempt as she elaborates her doctrine of the idealized self-image. This "self hatred" is essentially the same destructiveness which she has described in her earlier writings as sadistic and despairing, when it is turned against the self. It corresponds to masochistic trends.

The self-accusations appear similar to normal guilt feelings. But they are greatly exaggerated. They are manifestations of despair. Their neurotic focus on externals indicates their true purpose, which is to protect the actual self from complete submersion in despair, from complete debilitation by the oppressive self-images. Hence, the self-accusations may assume every listener to be a jurist.

Horney's picture of despair depicts one who hates himself not simply because his self-reproach may be in part valid. Instead, he accuses himself because he hates himself.[8] One self-accusation may

7. *Ibid.,* p. 201.
8. *Neurosis and Human Growth* (New York: W. W. Norton & Co., Inc., 1950), pp. 128–29.

follow another. "He does not take revenge; therefore he is a weakling. He is vindictive; therefore he is a brute. He is helpful; therefore he is a sucker. He is not helpful; therefore he is a selfish pig." If he externalizes—or, in Freudian language, "projects"—his self-accusations then he may imagine everybody is imputing "ulterior motives to everything he does." This may be so real in his own mind that he resents others, thinking they are always unfair. "In defense he may wear a rigid mask so that nobody will guess from his facial expressions, his tone of voice, or his gestures what is going on within him." He may be unaware of such externalizations. "In his conscious mind then everybody is very nice. And only during the analytic process will he realize that he actually feels under constant suspicion. Like Damocles, he may live in terror lest the sword of some severe accusation fall on him at any moment."[9]

Horney takes up where she feels Erich Fromm (in *Man for Himself*) leaves off too soon in his analysis of K in Kafka's *The Trial*. We may be inclined to extend her criticism to the K in *The Castle*, although that K takes a somewhat stronger initiative. Fromm points to the lack of autonomy, the dullness in K's drifting, guilty existence. K is always looking for someone else to solve his problems instead of turning to his own resources. He *should* feel the guilt which is projected in the form of a continually imminent trial, says Fromm, because he is guilty. The guilt is precisely that which has already been suggested in our study, especially by Kierkegaard. It is his failure to accept the strait and narrow, the anxious gate that opens to being himself—authentic involvement in the life that is possible.

But in her own literary diagnosis of K, Horney focuses on K's very attitude toward his guilt. It is unconstructive because he is dealing with it "in the spirit of self-hate," although the self-hate is not apparent.

Despairing guilt and/or shame is self-hatred. At its base, self-hatred is "neurotic pride," according to Horney. It is castigation of that self which has been rejected by the self which aspires to

9. *Ibid.*, p. 129.

acceptability and glory.[10] The person who is propelled by "neurotic pride" may seem the very personification of what the Greeks call *hubris*. Actually, however, he is a victim of society's sin. Self-accusation tries to rid the self of its perhaps "real" image. It inveighs against the mirrored likeness in the name of the romantic portrait painting which it fails to resemble. Neurotic pride smashes the mirror and sees the self only as the portrait.

Hubris—the kind of pride which in Greek tragedy asserts itself against the gods—refuses to accept the implications of the underlying anxiety, specifically, the facts of dependence and relationship, along with the potential for individuation. Denied most consciously, defiantly, is the desire—and need—for union. This is the "despair of defiance"—to use Kierkegaard's terminology.[11]

In her last book, Horney again discusses both resignation and destructiveness patterns. To the alcoholics and to Hedda Gabler she adds the State in George Orwell's *1984* as conveying what she sees as the self-demolishing potential of the oppressive idealized images.[12]

Self-pity may at times be a warning against the fall into despair. The actual self may be protesting, "Unfair!" This may well be the case when such self-pity appears in dreams. Again, we are reminded of the dream-like tales of Franz Kafka. Horney would agree with both Freud and Jung and definitely with the existential analysts, but in her own way: "In dreams," she says, "we are closer to the reality of ourselves."[13]

Horney closes her discussion of self-hatred with this eloquent statement: "Surveying self-hate and its ravaging force, we cannot help but see in it a great tragedy of the human mind." The person who has become dominated by his idealized self-image, "reaching out for the Infinite and Absolute" has started destroying himself.

---

10. *Ibid.*, pp. 130–32.

11. *The Sickness Unto Death*, pp. 200–207.

12. *Neurosis and Human Growth*, pp. 148–54.

13. *Ibid.*, pp. 152–53. If Horney is right here, then we should place new constructions on the phenomenon of self-pity, viz., that it is "half scandal." More accurately, we would have to say, authentic self-pity is the expression of an inner protest against despair. It is an expression of love for humanity —*my* humanity.

"When he makes a pact with the devil, who promises him glory, he has to go to hell—to the hell within himself."[14] This is the hell from which depth psychologists as therapists make it their business to save their patients and clients.

Absolute despair is the last precipice. Depth psychology, especially as actual therapy, recognizes utter hopelessness, regardless of how it manifests itself, as the last stop before either suicide or a psychotic break with reality. Horney follows her discussion of the more accessible despair, with a description of "self-alienation." This term is expanded to apply to conditions short of amnesias, depersonalizations, and other distortions. The nerves are cut, so to speak, between "the real self" and its front to the world "the actual self," and the latter becomes increasingly lost in its fictions.[15]

We recall the Freudian observations which lead to ideas of the splitting of the ego and the Kleinian conceptions of fragmented images incorporated from infancy on. We begin to appreciate Jung's complex diagram of selfhood and his and Otto Rank's respect for the irrational.

Harry Stack Sullivan interprets psychosis as a falling back into "prototaxic modes" of perceiving and behaving. He also sees the "self-system" as divided into dissociated "selves" each considering the others as "not me."[16]

Karen Horney equates the loss of the real self with what Kierkegaard called "the sickness unto death." Yet hopelessness is sickness, not death, but moving toward death, death, that is, to the real self, the potential that has been given to the human soul— the *psyche*.[17] Theologians go farther than the depth psychologists and speak of the death of the possibility of "essential humanity." "Despair" moves in depth through intensifications of guilt, of shame, of anxiety, toward utter distrustfulness.

Certainly, at this point in our discussion, the influence of

14. *Ibid.,* p. 154.
15. *Ibid.,* pp. 155 f.
16. See Mullahy, *Oedipus: Myth and Complex* (New York: Grove Press, 1955), p. 294.
17. Jung correlates psyche and *psyche* ("soul" in theology): "The Modern Spiritual "Problem," in *Modern Man in Search of a Soul,* Harvest Books edition (New York: Harcourt, Brace, 1933), pp. 201–2 and *passim.*

theorists like Ronald D. Laing (*The Divided Self,* and later works) is highly relevant. He should be read along with the earlier contemporary Anton T. Boisen (*The Exploration of the Inner World*). However, we cannot take time here to review or debate the controversy such thinking about psychosis introduces into our forum. The chief relevance for our inquiry is the question behind such a concept as self-alienation. Laing's point is that the alienation is against the sick society; there may be more health and movement toward health in the so-called schizophrenic, for instance, than there is in the society to which he is responding, or against which he is reacting. Furthermore many analysts would agree that there is a psychotic component in most every individual consciousness. Moreover, are not dreams themselves often like the awake reveries of the psychotic? The consensus insight seems to be that everyone has his psychotic defenses—or lookouts—along the boundary between himself and the outside world. The despair here may be a despair of the outside world, perhaps not despair of the inner world. However, insofar as one identifies him*self* (the inner world or much of it) with that despair, we can agree with Horney, that "self-alienation" is a form of hopelessness.

Little wonder, therefore, that theology—not only Christian theology—insists like an ever-tolling bell that the alternative is faith as trustfulness. However, can such a message be based on the analysis of despair? Indeed the strength and charm of the Christian evangel has been its conviction that there is ample reason for a new birth from despair into trustfulness. Has the grace of trustworthiness—trustworthy grace—come into the world for all mankind? This is the proclamation—if it can still be read through all the smoke of the illusions that hamper the heralds. The question must be directed to the heralds and theologians: In what way does this basic trustworthiness take form in the existence of persons and their society here and now, what is its *Gestalt*?[18]

Leaving so large a question to theologians, we return to the common ground: the state of soul in the individual. Is the

---

18. Cf. Paul Tillich, "The Formative Power of Protestantism," in *The Protestant Era* (Chicago: The University of Chicago Press, 1948), pp. 206–21. *Gestalt* refers to "the total structure of a living reality." (p. 206n.)

answer to the problem of despair, in some sense, that which was given to Nicodemus? "Back to the womb! You must be born again, established in a pattern of basic trustfulness. You must know what it is to be loved, to be in symbiotic union." The prescription is not that one must be reunited to "the mother" without ensuing separation. He must go through that trauma again, but with a renewal of trustfulness, a new venture through the narrow gate of anxiety.

Ian Suttie, Oskar Pfister, Horney, and Rank, along with the others make love the agent. It is at least analogous to the love-as-*agape* of the theologians, from St. Paul to the present day. In another biblical figure, the despairing one must be lifted up out of the miry clay and have his feet set upon a rock; he must have his way established.[19]

According to theologians, the salvation (*soteria*) is deliverance from the Janus-faced despair into which one may fall: despair of one's individuality and despair of belonging to the community. More profoundly, perhaps, it is deliverance from that despair which refuses to take the risk of existential anxiety. Such refusal may express itself in a variety of ways: avoidance, resignation, destructiveness, alcoholism, drug-addiction, and so forth. The "love of God in Christ" (*agape tou Theou en Christo*) is supposed to enable the individual to face the question of meaning in his existence, the question of the narrow way which requires hope, anxious hope and initiative—not simply restful faith but work with fear and trembling. However, again we must leave the question to the makers of theology.

In depth psychology we find the conviction that despair is never final so long as there is life. Even suicidal fantasies show a wish to be born again.[20] The tendency these days in psychotherapy is to

19. Psalm 40.
20. Regarding suicide, a contrary view is that of Joachin Flescher, who says that although suicide is associated with return to the womb, the underlying cause is the "death instinct." ("The Primary Constellation in the Structure and Treatment of Psychoses," *Psychoanalytic Review*, 40 [1953], p. 214.) Cf. Dietrich Bonhöffer, *Ethics*, ed. Eberhard Betthge (New York: Macmillan & Co., 1955), p. 123; also, Clyde A. Holbrook, *Faith and Community* (New York: Harper & Row, 1959), pp. 18–19. Tillich, in *Systematic Theology*, Vol. 2, pp. 86–90, discusses the meaning of despair in terms of suicide and the symbols of "the wrath of God" and "condemnation."

regard no psychotic as completely inaccessible. Perhaps the so-called sociopathic and psychopathic are not inaccessible either. Of course the condition of those whose distress can be traced to organic brain damage or other physiological cause may pose another problem. Yet, even for them the "Gestalt of grace" should be at work on an answer. However, in those who are at all accessible to depth therapy despair need not be absolute. Nor must we settle for a kind of *fall out* of consciousness, whether into sensuality[21] or drug-induced euphoria, as the antidote.

The most resigned, the most destructive, the most despairing one is still in the game. Whereas despair cries, or moans, "Catastrophe has struck!", life itself seems to go on saying, "Perhaps some hope will come to me redemptively and save me from utter meaninglessness!" Merely continuing to exist says this much.

---

21. Reinhold Niebuhr discusses one form of *sin* as despairing escape into sensuality. (*The Nature and Destiny of Man,* Vol. 1 [New York: Charles Scribner's Sons, 1941–   ], pp. 228–40.) Karen Horney discusses sensuality as "a strategy" for avoiding the "basic anxiety." (*The Neurotic Personality of Our Time* (New York: W. W. Norton & Co., Inc., 1937), pp. 147–61.) Both sensuality and suicide—different though they may seem—can be studied in relation to the Freudian idea of regression (or regressive "solution" to present crisis). Certainly, they may be viewed in terms of the Rankian model of "individuation" and "relationship." (And, curiously, in Rank both the "average man" and "the neurotic" seem to be despairing types.)

10

Self-consciousness and World-consciousness

Even while using the Genesis story of the fall of man, theologians have tended to define both the cause and the state as self-centeredness, self-love, selfishness, self-conceit.[1] In our inquiry into depth psychology we must seek for correlation and corrective here, as well.

What is the phenomenon of self-concern? We see it in guilt feelings, shame feelings, anxiety states, and despair. Perhaps it is epitomized in the attitude which says in action if not words, "Myself right or wrong!" and "Myself always right!"

Classical Freudian thought gives pretty much the following description of self-love. It is "primary narcissism" augmented by "secondary narcissism." Borrowing the term from Havelock Ellis,[2] Freud views narcissism as erotic love for the self—the physical, organismic, biological, somatic self. Primary narcissism is considered as absolutely inevitable; it is in the nature of the case, implicit in being an organism. It is the organism's instinctual concern with its own satisfaction. Secondary narcissism is "erotic involvement with oneself resulting from interference in the development of the love impulse toward others," according to Clara Thompson's definition.[3] Freud speaks of this kind of narcissism when he construes a person's self-concern as tantamount to sexual attachment to his own body as though it were an outside object. The theory has been refined to mean attachment to one's own ego —what Paul Schilder would call "body ego."[4]

1. For but one of countless examples which we can find, Paul Ramsay: "*Sin* is anxious self-centeredness or self-centered anxiety." (*Basic Christian Ethics* [New York: Charles Scribner's Sons, 1954], p. 291.)
2. See Ellis, *The Psychology of Sex* (New York: New American Library, 1938), pp. 102–3.
3. *An Outline,* Thompson, et al., eds., p. 617.
4. *The Image and Appearance of the Human Body* (New York: International Universities Press, 1950). Besides Schilder's writings the psycho-

To Freud narcissism is the libidinal complement of what is popularly called egoism. Its force varies with the individual. A person may be markedly egoistic, but with a relatively strong libidinal attachment to outside objects. His narcissism is chiefly of the primary type. Another egoist may have a relatively strong libidinal attachment to himself, to his own body, body image.

In discussing narcissistic symptoms which may be marked even in normal persons especially during a situational neurosis, Freud says, "Certain conditions—organic illness, painful excesses of stimulation, an inflammatory condition of an organ—have clearly the effect of loosening the libido from its attachment to its objects. The libido which has thus been withdrawn attaches itself again to the ego in the form of a stronger investment of the diseased region of the body."[5]

As we read what Freud wrote both before and after he introduced the dualistic instincts theory, we get the impression that such elaborate descriptions of ego-dynamics are, at their base, attempts to systematize an unavoidable commonplace about the individual. He does seem to have ingrained self-concern. Perhaps this departs from him at the precipice of suicide. But even so, the logic is that it is coterminous only with life itself. Even when he loses himself in some great cause or, perhaps less nobly, in "sensuality" he carries with him some of this concern. Freud discusses the question, notably, in "Mourning and Melancholia":

> We have come to recognize a self-love of the ego which is so immense, in the fear that rises up at the menace of death we see liberated a volume of narcissistic libido which is so vast, that we cannot conceive how this ego can connive at its own destruction. . . . Now the analysis of melancholia shows that the ego can kill itself

---

analytic literature on "body ego" includes such titles as these: Sylvan Keiser, "Body Ego During Orgasm," *Psychoanalytic Quarterly* XXI (1952), pp. 153–66; and "House Construction Play, Its Interpretation and Diagnostic Value," *International Journal of Psycho-Analysis,* XXXIX (1958), pp. 39–49. One's house-concept is related to his three-dimensional body image, our way of representing our body to ourselves" (p. 39). Cf Ernest Jones, "Psycho-Analysis and the Instincts," in *Papers on Psycho-Analysis,* 4th ed. (London: Bailliere, 1938), p. 209.

5. *A General Introduction to Psycho-Analysis* trans. Joan Riviere (Garden City, N.Y.: Permabook, 1953), p. 426.

only when, the object-cathexis having been withdrawn upon it, it can treat itself as an object, when it is able to launch against itself the animosity relating to an object—that primordial reaction on the part of the ego to all objects in the outer world.[6]

After 1920, when Freud introduced the concept of a primitive death—or destructiveness—instinct, it is hardly accurate to assume that his explanation of self-love continued to be simply as it was stated with a presupposition of hedonic monism. However, he did not repudiate the earlier theories. After he posited an instinctual dualism Freud continued to assume that the so-called libidinal forces, the sexual, erotic "instincts" oppose the organism's bent toward death. As they persist in prolonging the journey toward it, they are narcissistic. As they attach to the ego as object—self-concept, they are narcissistic in the secondary sense.

As we have noted, *The Ego and the Id* set forth the new doctrine of ego structure. What happened to the notion of an ego ideal? There is some reason simply to assume that Freud intended to absorb it into his new doctrine of superego. Franz Alexander, an important spokesman for a dynamic application of Freudian analysis, is representative of many disciples when he insists that the ego ideal is still there in the structure of the ego. It is like an international organization, pervading both ego and superego.[7]

Freud says: "It would be possible to picture the id as under the domination of the mute but powerful death-instincts, which desire to be at peace and (as the pleasure-principle demands) to put Eros, the intruder, to rest; but that would be to run the risk of valuing too cheaply the part played by Eros."[8] And Eros plays a part in the ego ideal. However, in his final summing up, Freud is

6. "Mourning and Melancholia," (1917). In her revised translation, based on her earlier one in 1925, she uses "consent" instead of "connive." The last phrase in the passage we quoted was altered to read, "the ego's original reaction to objects in the external world." (*Complete Psychological Works*, Vol. 4, trans. Joan Riviere (London: Hogarth, 1957), p. 252.) See the earlier translation *A General Selection*, ed. John Richman (London: Hogarth, 1953), pp. 152–53.

7. Development of the Ego Psychology," *Imago*, XX (1934), *International Journal of Psycho-Analysis*, XVII, (1936), reprinted in Hendrik M. Ruiten-beek, ed., *Heirs to Freud* (New York: Grove Press, 1966), pp. 221–33, figure 2, especially.

8. *The Ego and the Id* (London: Hogarth, 1923), pp. 87–88.

still insisting that the superego is the internal agency which mobilizes and directs the death instincts in their unceasing assault on the ego.[9] Since, for him the superego is the seat of conscience, that famous inner voice is hardly to be regarded as narcissistic. What, then, is the force which Horney describes as the tyranny of the "should" and which Adler recognizes as superiority striving? Do these forces not characterize much of that behavior which is popularly labeled "egoism?"

Freud relates pre-verbal autistic thinking to the phenomenon. The infant has what he calls "omnipotence" feelings and fantasies. In an intriguing little paper, written before he arrived at his instinctual dualism, Freud describes three historic occasions—or movements—which have wounded the narcissism, or self-love, of mankind. In his list of three we perceive an intertwining of self- with world-consciousness! The three historic crises were: (1) cosmological (Copernicus), (2) biological (Darwin), and (3) psychological (we infer Freud, although he mentions Schopenhauer "whose unconscious 'Will' is equivalent to the instincts in the mind as seen by psycho-analysis").[10]

Scientific psychology is making progress these days in learning more about the world of the infant. Much of the scientific reporting seems, to confirm an early interpolative judgment of Melanie Klein. "I believe," she says, "that babies have altogether more intellectual capacity than is assumed."[11] To be sure, the infant has no developed concept of himself as differentiated from the milieu. Psychologically, therefore, he continues in a quasi-symbiotic state. Events simply happen in his world after the trauma of separation from the body of his mother. He is hungry; he is fed. He is cold; he is warmed. Nurture and biological satisfaction along with occasional privation are for the normal infant the formative experiences through which he makes his way in what may be called the "dawn of consciousness." Objects and persons gradually do emerge from the field. He grasps them, withdraws from them, and

9. *An Outline,* pp. 92, 112 f.
10. *Collected Papers,* Vol. 4 (London: Hogarth, 1956), pp. 347–56, at p. 355. (*Complete Psychological Works,* Vol. 17.)
12. Klein, "Weaning," in John Rickman, ed., *On Bringing Up Children* (London: Kegan Paul, Trench & Trubner, 1938), pp. 54–55.

relates himself to them in varying ways. Some of them he assimilates within his own psychic world. Others he rejects, resists, sometimes without success, since they may be imposed on him. The autistic mode of thinking, the mode of "prototaxis" according to Harry Stack Sullivan, is probably what one is re-experiencing, resorting to perhaps, when he is drawn by "magic." It is the matrix for belief in magic. Perhaps this helps explain such phenomena as hypnosis and the magnetic pull of some mass evangelists, not to mention salesmen. Jungian concepts of extroversion and introversion are both apropos.[12]

The understanding of primary self-concern and autism bears directly on the *hubris* described by theologians and theorists like Horney when she speaks of the pride system. It also may shed light on the more overtly affectional forms of self-love and the covert forms in which the persisting underlying concern defends the self against the threats of starvation, separation, and abandonment. It is that deep motivation for warding off censure, rejection, and privation. It is that which says: "I must be satisfied, secure, right at all costs—at least right in the sense of being 'right' in order to be secure ('all right'). I am what I am. I want what I want when I want it. I must be in a position to endure—and if need be, to conquer—this or that situation."

To say that this aspect of human nature is sinfulness in its essence would be, it seems to me, rather unenlightening. It is true we do not like selfishness especially as we see it in others. Freud himself seemed to be intolerant of narcissism in his colleagues and others.[13] Yet, the omnipotence feeling and the patterning of behavior which one sees in unattractive selfishness and egoism are logically no more blameworthy than object-adoring, rather than self-as-object-adoring, behavior. Object-adoring may well be object-consuming. We remember Uncle Screwtape, in C. S. Lewis'

12. Cf. "ego-centrism": its cause and its effect on learning, as seen by Jean Piaget. The egocentric child is a neglected child, in not being properly introduced to other centers of interest (*The Language and Thought*, 2nd ed. [1930], trans. Marjorie Gabain [New York: Meridian Books, 1955]).
13. Secondary narcissism, we assume, is the weakness that Freud finds hard to take. See Ernest Jones, "Obituary of Hanns Sach," *The International Journal of Psycho-Analysis,* XXVII (1946), pp. 168–69.

idea of the demonic, who could close his letters to his nephew Wormwood with both "Your affectionate uncle," and "Ravenously yours."[14] The egoist who loves others as objects more than himself-as-object may actually be far more dangerous than the person who is lost in erotic self-appreciation. The latter is more like a vegetable. The former is like a ravenous beast.

The "urge to grow" which Horney describes, the "self" with its life force, depicted by Jung, the counter-will which Rank features, and what Suttie describes under "solipsism,"[15] and Sullivan's "waking self" within the "self system" all assume what we call "self-concern" as intrinsic to human nature. Indeed it would precede any fall into consciousness. If, then, it is to be construed as sin by theologians, it is entirely appropriate—if not very enlightening—to posit sin as with man in his garden even before the fall into the knowledge of good and evil.

Indeed with the Apostle Paul we may say that man makes of himself a sinner by his own rationalizing of the state he finds himself in. At least, this seems to be something like what Paul is saying in a perhaps isolated passage, if we think of Judaic law—the law of Moses—as the product of what we have labeled rationalizing. "Sin indeed was in the world before the law was given, but sin is not counted where there is no law."[16] To be sure, Paul is the primal theologian in Christendom who uses Adam as the model for our sinful condition. Paul's Christ, on the other hand, is the new Adam—the Adam who transgressed "was a type of the one who was to come." But that is another story, although not at all irrelevant to our inquiry, this Pauline answer to what we have called the "fall into consciousness"—which, however, is not quite his construction on what happened in Eden.

Probably the depth psychologists are right in seeing self-love and self-seeking—arrogance and egoism as well—as symptomatic of infantile deprivation. The infant and small child has had to

14. *The Screwtape Letters* (New York: Macmillan & Co., 1945).
15. Ian Suttie, objecting to Freud's hypothesis of a primary "narcissism," prefers what he calls a primary solipsism, marked simply by the inability to discriminate between the "self" and the "other." (*The Origins of Love and Hate* (London: Kegan Paul, 1935), pp. 30 ff.
16. Rom: 5:13.

retreat into himself or else fixate on object relations that are less than the best for his future development.[17]

A love-of-self which is irreducible is implicit in the human as well as other creatures. To call it ingrained wrongness would simply be to decry the species. Perhaps all biological life is one grand mistake. But where can such negativity take us? Yet it is possible to talk in terms of health and illness. There is such a thing as unhealthy self-love.

Why should one assume responsibility in society, yes, at times even blame for this or that state of affairs? True, it is possible for one to assume too much guilt, presupposing an unrealistic degree of freedom and responsibility in the affairs of the world. Implicit in the very fact of consciousness—self-consciousness and world-consciousness—is an answer to our question: the waking self insists on assuming responsibility for the navigation of the vastly irrational psyche. Guilt feelings when viewed as a dynamism behave almost like a faculty. They reveal that there is within the individual a will to be free, to be in charge.

By definition also the individual is in relationship. This is true even if he becomes physically isolated. Psychologically he is in relationship. The behaviorists also would agree that consciousness —in its very nature, with words and images and tones of voice— is social, interpersonal. The person who all alone is talking to himself, or simply musing, is talking with someone, musing about and in the presence of someone or some many within his socially produced inner forum.

In other words, most consciousness assumes a dialogue, even if that dialogue is completely internalized. Perhaps, we should say psychologically internalized.

Indeed much consciousness can be described as interpersonal suffering in isolation. Conscious mulling over the past, projecting into the future, and rehearsal in the present are work, the I in "I am conscious" piloting the self in the interpersonal field. It is little wonder then that mystical and religious programs of salvation

17. For illustration of the point, see O. Spurgeon English and Gerald N. J. Pearson, *Emotional Problems of Living* (New York: W. W. Norton & Co., Inc., 1945), pp. 26–27 and *passim*.

try to liberate the subject-self from such concern with pilotage. Why not just sit back and relax? Let the self be the self without the pain of self-consciousness. Various kinds of self-mysticism are available east and west in discursive and creative writing and in other media. Perhaps Jungian psychology comes closest, among those we have considered, to de-emphasizing the ego[18]—but there the use of the term is qualitatively different from that in Freudian and other theory.

Should psychotherapy relieve one from suffering and the strenuosness of trying to master his own fate? Instead of trying so hard can the sufferer take it easy? Can such liberation be without the loss of consciousness? In other words, can one participate with some confidence, and perhaps joy, in the experience of consciousness?

Some would depict the optimal state as being carried along on a powerful current; it is mysterious like a dream. To be sure, the subject must think and do, although some forms of religious, mystical, or psychotherapeutic salvation suggest rather more of one than of the other.

In Western religion, generally, the trouble with the human species has been diagnosed not only as selfishness but also as idolatry. The fall of man was a fall into idolatry, placing his objects and concepts in the role of God; adoring mere things, even other human beings, more than God.

Depth psychology of the infant and the young child also weakens this time-honored reduction of sin to idolatry. Idolatry is analogous to, if not psychologically derived from, the individual's relation to objects from the very beginning of his interaction with his environment. Idolatry, like egoism, harks back to the child's understanding of the environment which discloses itself to him, of the objects and images which are its very countenance—smiling, frowning, expressionless. His world is physiognomic.[19]

18. Cf. Erich Neumann's entirely Jungian construction on the "evolution" of "ego consciousness." (*The Origins and History of Consciousness*, Vol. 1, trans. R. F. C. Hull (New York: Harper Torchbooks, 1962), p. 36.
19. See Heinz Werner, *The Comparative Psychology of Mental Development* (New York: Harper & Row, 1940), p. 262, and the discussion of Werner's "physiognomic" stage in Gardner Murphy, *Personality: A Bio-*

Furthermore, if we follow, at least part of the way, Melanie Klein and Ronald Fairbairn, and view the ego as being constituted by its objects—split images and all the rest—perhaps we can say that the self-image of every person includes the *objective* visage of his society, especially that which bore in upon him during his so-called formative years. And there is much to be said—à la Marshall McLuhan, for instance, and in different vein, the ego psychologists, revisionists, and existential analysts—for the conviction that this self-identifying process continues: "All that I have met is a part of *me*"—if we may rephrase a line from Tennyson's *Ulysses.*

What are the inferences for man in a changing, shrinking world which at the same time grows more complicated? What are the inferences for his social and spiritual health? In response to this question let us venture a homely construction, or reconstruction, which may be suggestive.

If the ego is constituted of its objects—its images of its environment (although, it is true a psychotic may come to think "I am a television set"), then the self-image of every person in a bi-racial, or multi-racial society includes in its mosaic more than the race of his "racial origin." In other words, psychologically, a southern white man who as a child identified with significant persons (Sullivan) who were black (cook, baby-sitter, janitor at the school —just to name a few examples of roles which are somewhat frequent in the recent south), perhaps being under the authority of black significant persons, this white man is also a black man. Indeed such a white man is, in his self-concept which reaches deep into his unconscious, a white man, black man, white woman, and black woman. By the same token, the black man is also a white man, psychologically speaking.

Since the habit has been for the white to regard the black as

---

social *Approach to Origins and Structure* (New York: Harper & Row, 1947), pp. 266, 268, 336, 358, 365, 387, and 994. See also Werner's revised edition of his book (Chicago: Follett, 1948), pp. 382–83 and *passim.* Also, regarding the physiognomic factor, see Harry Stack Sullivan, *The Interpersonal Theory of Psychiatry*, ed. Helen Swick Perry and Mary Ladd Gawel (New York: W. W. Norton & Co., Inc., 1953), pp. 145–48.

inferior, the "white man" has tended to suppress, or indeed *re*press, his identification with the black significant persons in his life. And the black man has felt constrained to suppress his own identification with his white significant persons. When persons are free from the bondage of such repressions so that they can practice the kind of self-awareness and world-awareness that discerns the mosaic of both black and white, then perhaps there can be more of a psychological and spiritual solution to the problem which is labeled "race."

Perhaps, also, there can be a rediscovery of conscience with the help of thinking like that of our panel in this inquiry. If the ego is constituted by its objects and significant persons then it may include within it a construct or a whole constellation of images and notions of order, goodness, and love, which corresponds to an ideal such as "the Kingdom of God" and which is defined in universal humanitarian ways. It is, or would be, like a higher tribunal in the inner government of the mind. To be sure, the structure of the invisible mind is still veiled in mystery, despite all our analogizing insights—Freudian, Jungian, Rankian and the rest. We may even decide to throw up our hands and convert to the behaviorists like B. F. Skinner and say that such speculation is, if not beside the point, not edifying—because of the inaccessibility of 'hard factual data.'[20]

However, our inquiry has been speculative, dealing with speculative minds among psychologists and theologians. Indeed we could go even further with some of them—doubtless some would part company with us—and look at systems of psychology and philosophy which allow for presentational[21] as well as representational unconscious thinking and thus for something like yet another, and perhaps prior conscience. Both Rank and Horney would stay on for such a session, as would Jung, certainly. Freud's doctrine of phylogenetic superego is certainly a notion of innate conscience. Fairbairn's theory that there are as many egos as there are internalized objects (images), with a central ego in their midst, along with

---

20. Cf. *Beyond Freedom and Dignity* (New York: Alfred A. Knopf, 1971).
21. Cf., Ernst Cassirer; and Susanne K. Langer, *Philosophy in a New Key* (New York: Mentor Books, 1948).

an internal collective saboteur, suggests still another model that may possibly be useful to us as we try to search out the mystery of conscience or consciences. We have also mentioned philosophers and theologians who assume a doctrine of a transcendent conscience and also of a self-transcending self, which so far the psychologists have not been able to elucidate.

The problem of finding a higher conscience distinct from both the society-relative and the individual-relative conscience is a question that refuses to leave the forum of both academic and practical discourse. For but one, yet significant example, we think of H. Richard Niebuhr's writings, especially *Christ and Culture* and *The Meaning of Revelation,* not forgetting his brother's *Moral Man in Immoral Society* and *An Interpretation of Christian Ethics.*

If we read theologians who make a radical disjunction between old Adamic and new Adamic consciousness, we find ourselves not only in the presence of Paul of Tarsus but also close to the Sigmund Freud who wrote *Civilization and Its Discontents.* These theologians say in effect that there is nothing in mankind or his situation "apart from the grace of God" that offers anything that warrants labels such as redemption, *agape,* or hope. The *imago dei* (man created in the image of God) is broken, shattered. All that man has from his history is refracted images, mostly in bits and pieces. But one of them makes all the difference: that is the Word (*logos*) made flesh. Freud, of course, would not be at home with the theological language. However, his assessment of human nature is not too far from that of these theologians.

Paul Lehmann and others, notably Karl Barth, see the dynamics of the Christ symbolism as it offers to redeem fallen mankind, as event, encounter, redemptive act in history. This *history* is of ideas, institutions, society, man and nature. After being confronted with the gospel of "the Word made flesh," the encountered man beholds the world with new lenses, we may call them context lenses. This, as I understand it, is the kind of emphasis we find in contextual theology.[22]

22. See, for example, Paul Lehmann, *Ethics in a Christian Context* (New York: Harper & Row, 1963). Incidentally, Professor Lehmann includes a perceptive treatment of Freud's contribution to the study of "conscience."

What would depth psychology say to such a new consciousness? Of course Freudians would be able to offer their doctrinal instruments including ego mechanisms: identification, introjection, projection, sublimation, and all the rest. Jungians would speak of "symbols of transformation."[23]

"Theologians of hope" are getting a hearing these days. And process theology is another method that continues to be taken seriously. Without exploring the matter of comparative theology at this point, we can at least hear the consensus voice of that long tradition which has at times been labeled natural theology. For instance, Daniel Day Williams says, "Christianity believes in man more deeply than any other historic faith. . . . Life in all its struggle is good at the core."[24]

Edgar P. Dickie, who along with Donald M. Baillie, helped me understand the life-affirmative tendencies in Christian theology, would say that the "new consciousness" defines the "old." Only on the side of "grace" can one see what theologians have called the "sinfulness of sin."[25]

The grace about which all these theologians speak must have a gestalt. Some may emphasize the mystery of grace as it comes when and where one expects it not. "God moves in a mysterious way his wonders to perform." Others, notably theologians kin to the Karl Barth of *Church Dogmatics*, may emphasize the form which the grace takes in the *kerygma* (the message of Christianity) and, most importantly, the *koinonia* (community of the new consciousness). Perhaps it is not merely coincidental that the "grace" finds institutional expression. These theologians would be quick to point out, however, that the grace and the institutional expression must be carefully distinguished from each other. Tillich's phrase "catholic substance and protestant principle" still seems, to my mind, to be about the best succinct summary of this critical point.

---

23. The phrase "symbols of transformation" is the title of the 1952 revision of Jung's "The Psychology of the Unconscious" and is volume 5 of *Collected Works of C. G. Jung* (London: Routledge and Kegan Paul, and New York: Bolingen Foundation [Bollingen Series XX, Vol. 7], 1953).

24. *What Present Day Theologians Are Thinking* (New York: Harper & Row, 1952), p. 149.

25. *God Is Light* (London: Hodder and Stoughton, 1953), p. 13.

Self-love is still a problem for anyone who is concerned with causes larger than his own happiness. In the mid-1950's an exchange between a revisionist psychoanalyst and a philosophical theologian, Erich Fromm and Paul Tillich, centered on this question. Tillich took exception to Fromm's advocacy of self-love, in *The Sane Society*. Tillich argued that self-affirmation or self-acceptance would be less ambiguous. Fromm defended his terminology. He even appealed to Tillich's favorite authority, the biblical conceptions. There is a proper self-love implicit in the love commandment: "Thou shalt love thy neighbor *as* thyself." Fromm is arguing for a kind of self-transcendence in which one can look on oneself as a person, even as he can regard others as persons outside himself. Such a self-transcendence seems to be characteristic of human self-consciousness anyway. Fromm contends that selfishness—as distinguished from self-concern—is really self-hatred. Correlating his doctrine with Horney's we can say that selfishness is a form of despair, or an attempt to escape from the opportunity to be oneself. The selfish person is a victim of a deep inner hopelessness. Fromm illustrates his point with Peer Gynt's devotion to self. He lost the self which he sought. Love of things and fancies, grasping for objects, selfishly, is actually rejecting one's real self.

Of course, the skeptic, armed with his own interpretation of the kind of object-psychology we find in Klein and Fairbairn, may well say to Fromm and Horney: there is no real self beyond its *object*ification. To avoid such an impasse we may need Buber with his corrective which distinguishes between I-it and I-Thou relationships. Peer Gynt was collecting I-it relationships until he himself became a mere it. In Peer Gynt, "To thyself be true" was twisted and lost in a way of life that read, "To thyself be enough."[26] He "thingified" himself.

26. Fromm, *Man for Himself* (London: Routledge and Kegan Paul, 1949), pp. 119–40. The references to the Tillich-Fromm exchanges are: Tillich, "Erich Fromm's *The Sane Society*," *Pastoral Psychology*, VI (56), (September 1955), p. 14; Fromm, *The Art of Loving* (New York: Harper & Row, 1956), p. 57n.
Fromm, in *The Sane Society* (New York: Rinehart, 1955), takes to task not only Calvin and Luther but also Immanuel Kant for confusing "selfishness" with "self-love."

To the extent that such an attitude—such a response to the call of anxiety, the Janus-faced anxiety depicted by Otto Rank—is a free choice then it can be regarded as accountable. But by the same token if one has chosen to despair he may therefore be open to being convinced that he was wrong in his choice—of his sin— and moved to change his heading. In the long run—from birth to death—is there any substantial basis for an alternative to such despair with oneself? The alternative, according to Christian teaching, is to accept the grace of basic trustworthy love (*agape*). It is reasonable of course for one to inquire: Where is it?

The problem of guilt and responsibility, even when it is not reduced to such concepts as idolatry and self-love, is existential for man as a social being. It is worth noting, incidentally, that although Freud intended to argue against religion—as growth-stunting illusion, he argued strongly for assuming responsibility. And he was almost preoccupied with the determinative power of guilt feeling. In his, *The Future of An Illusion,* especially, he expressed his own credo in reason: the ego as intelligence. In *Civilization and Its Discontents,* he added the tenet *eros* to his statement of faith, expressing a hope, not a firm belief:

> The fateful question for the human species seems to me to be whether and to what extent their cultural development will succeed in mastering the disturbance of their communal life by the human instinct of aggression and self-destruction . . . Men have gained control over the forces of nature to such an extent that with their help they would have no difficulty in exterminating one another to the last man. They know this, and hence . . . their mood of anxiety. And now it is to be expected that the other of the two 'Heavenly Powers,' external Eros, will make an effort to assert himself in the struggle with his equally immortal adversary.[27]

After the book was published, and when he saw the star of Hitler rising, he seemed to waver even in so tentative a faith and added to this final sentence a new one: "But who can foresee with what success and with what result?" (1931).

In principle, the alternative to despair is hope as the triumph of trustfulness. The mature individual who chooses to hope rather

27. *Civilization and Its Discontents,* in *Complete Psychological Works,* p. 145.

than to despair will be more than egocentric; he will be more than self-conscious. "The Kingdom of God" can become a focus for consciousness. At best, however, the individual will have two foci of concern: himself—such is the nature of the species—and "the Kingdom of God." Some readers may prefer other symbols: community, a better world, the new humanity, or simply, others.

Although the person has no choice in the matter of intrinsic self-concern nor in much of the twisting of that concern by a nightmarish introduction to the world of objects and events, his accountable offense is in the supposed interest of his self-concern or in despair of that interest. We can cite the legend of Adapa or of Gilgamesh, and many others from archaic lore on, but the readiest of these for our Western spectacles is probably the story with which we began this book, Adam and Eve in the garden of Eden. The story of their fall into consciousness—often rendered, fall into sin—suggests that the one who tempted them, "the serpent" was some outside or transcendent evil force or principle. Did it deceive their self-concern into choosing a way of despair over a way of hope? If so, then the deception came in the very guise of hope.

But can we suppose that for mankind there may have been an alternate route? In any case, he finds himself discerning his situation as though he were above it, up there somewhere looking down on himself—a glorious pitiful creature.

The problem which man has with himself is the inevitable concomitant of intelligence. In our determination to be conscious of the world and of ourselves we insist on acquiring yet more knowledge. And we know our limitations! Indeed much of our projecting of our knowledge—and our extending of it—into the world relates to this consciousness of our own limitations.

We extend ourselves into machines and technology increasingly complex. We may be headed toward a time when we can program our*selves* (or at least our intelligences) into forms that are not perishable. I think of that rectangular slab in Arthur C. Clarke's' *2001*: "A Space Odyssey."[28] In the Freudian frame of reference

28. A Signet book, New American Library, 1968.

'it shall be brought to pass the saying': "where id was there shall ego be"!—ego as intelligence or intellect. Or, if we prefer to switch over to B. F. Skinner's behaviorist frame of reference, we may say that 'the day cometh' when we shall have truly "de-homunculized"[29] ourselves and won through to a new humanity—although the millennium may come about by means other than those which Skinner prescribes. Alas, this takes us into another important debate. And we must call time for now. But before we do we should note that the import of the arguments of both the behaviorists and the depth psychologists is that through the use of his intelligence man must work out his own salvation! And who would deny that he has not yet won through to salvation? Indeed if he is to survive as a species he must hasten to build a realistic paradise to the East of Eden. "With God's help!" urge the theologians. But they, even Karl Barth, can talk about the *humanity* of God.[30] Even the antiphonal complement offered by theologians is a transcendent humanism. Yes, the very genius of the best in Christian theology—and in certain other theology—is this humanism, "the new humanity!"

Consciousness is work! And we can do this kind of work with nostalgia for the autistic paradise we left behind. Freud and his successors speak of the dream work. We can call consciousness—including that which is "unconscious" as in the dream—*play* as well as work, for in the last analysis they are two modes of the same theme: man's self-conscious, world-conscious coping with nature and time.

29. Skinner's terminology—*Beyond Freedom and Dignity.*
30. Cf. Karl Barth, *The Humanity of God,* trans. John N. Thomas and Thomas Wieser (Richmond: John Knox Press, 1960).

Index of Names and Subjects